C000253791

Published by:
Perissos Media
Northern Ireland, UK
Ask us for a FREE book on publishing your message to the world:
www.PerissosGroup.com/support

Edited by: Margaret Buckley

ISBN-13: 978-0-9926677-6-4

For more information on the work of Michael S Fryer, please visit:

www.FathersHouse.wales

Contents

Preface

Seventy years after the mass murder of the Jews of Europe, Holocaust denial and Holocaust revisionism are creeping into our overall picture of what actually happened. Facts and figures are manipulated and diminished in order to make the Holocaust less important and even to attempt to suggest that the Jews themselves were to blame. All these things are a betrayal of the truth of course and they taint the memory and history of the atrocities of the Shoah/Holocaust.

Each group in society decides how much, if any, of their memory of the events which led to the mass murder of Jews is tainted by the lies perpetrated today by those motivated by anti-Semitism. The Holocaust denials of Iranian Leaders or the academic denials of those who, like the historian David Irving, all attempt to create a narrative which questions the facts surrounding the Shoah.

Christendom has not denied Holocaust but has attempted to create a memory of Holocaust which suggests that the Christians of Europe were, without exception, rescuers of Jews or knew nothing about the mass murders. Many of Christendom's leaders today are promoting Holocaust exhibitions and Holocaust study and all that is good, but what many do not understand is that Christendom not only fuelled the hatred of Jews prior to the war years, but actually played an active role in intensifying hatred against the Jews of Europe. Christians and their Clergy even took an active part in the murder of Jews, particularly during the early years of the War when millions of Jews were shot in the communities in which they lived.

My studies, over many years, have led me to believe that this rose tinted memory of Holocaust has led us in Christendom, to believe that we are not responsible in any way for the genocide known as Holocaust and it has placed us in a position whereby we are unable to learn from the past enabling the possibility of us repeating it. Repeating our hatred of Jews has been a re-occurring factor in the history of the relentless persecution of the Jews.

This book has been written in a way which highlights a number of events which will help the reader form some conclusions about the involvement and motives of Christians in Europe in the years prior to and during World War Two. Not every country in German Occupied territory has been discussed in this book as research of Christian involvement in those countries is not finished and in some cases has only just begun.

Much of the evidence I have presented in this book has been taken from the writings of those eminent historians who have spent their lives gathering evidence and researching the truth about events in Holocaust. Some of these historians are survivors and some are children of survivors, but all are committed to bringing the truth about this stain on our society into the open.

The evidence these eminent scholars and researchers have presented and the material which I use as a foundation for my thesis on Christian complicity, has been verified and corroborated in many ways both through historic records and archive material, some of which is available in the archives at Yad Vashem - the Holocaust Memorial Trust.

Holocaust Survivor and Author Primo Levi wrote: "Those who deny Auschwitz would be ready to remake it"

Today we see Christian organisations, Churches and Church leaders vilify Israel and condemn its right to exist. Is this in part because they have denied Christendom's role in the tragedy we call Holocaust?

Mike Fryer

Acknowledgments

When I began my life as a police officer, I had no idea that my investigative skills and desire for truth would have led me to research the most despicable of all crimes, the Holocaust. The perpetrators of this terrible crime numbered in their thousands and the victims in their millions. Witnesses are numbered in their multi-millions.

Many of those who mentored me in my detective career were diligent investigators who sought truth. They helped me to follow this lifestyle of crime investigation in many areas, including drugs, murder, child abuse and major criminals.

I am grateful to these mentors, because the skills that they taught me have helped me in my investigations into Christian complicity in Holocaust. This lead to my conclusion that Christendom conspired in the murder of Jews prior to and during Holocaust.

Since retiring from the National Crime Squad, I have graduated in Holocaust Studies from Yad Vashem, the Holocaust Memorial. I am truly thankful to those who sponsored my studies and to those academics such as Ephraim and Stephanie Kay, Professors Robert Wistrich, Franklyn H Little, Yehuda Baur and many other academics serving on the Yad Vashem team. These men and women helped me to understand that Holocaust could not be understood from a human standpoint. I am also grateful to the amazing authors who wrote the papers and books which formed the foundation of my understanding

I also want to thank my congregation, Father's House Sabbath Congregation in North Wales, whose members have not only released me to study but have also supported and encouraged me to carry on with my studies. They are a wonderful congregation and I can't thank them enough.

Finally I want to thank Shirley my wife, and Grace and Samuel, my children, who have given me the time and encouragement to spend time away in study and time at home reading and researching the large number of books and materials. Their love and patience in response to my repeating my findings over and over again can only be described as amazing.

Chapter 1 ~ Memories

THE GENOCIDE known as the Holocaust, or 'Shoah' to the Jews, is probably the most remembered of all genocides. Library history shelves are packed with books about World War II and Holocaust studies. Thousands of testimonies, books, exhibitions, films, plays, university courses, school syllabuses, museums and memorials all ensure that the memory of the Holocaust is not lost. Holocaust memorials such as the Yad Vashem museum in Jerusalem, where I graduated in Holocaust studies, are an amazing resource of material which will ensure that the memory of this terrible period in our history will never be forgotten.

Memory, however, is selective, dependent on individual proclivities. Victims' memories will be different to that of the perpetrator. We value greatly the thousands of testimonies given by survivors in pursuit of what happened. Survivors who lost families and suffered greatly are vital in the recording of genocide truths. Their memory is likely to be far more accurate than that of a perpetrator who has a motive for blanking out the cruelty of what happened.

The value of survivors' memory was illustrated in a Parliamentary debate during the 1991 War Crimes Bill. This became an Act of Parliament, allowing the investigation and prosecution of war criminals who had murdered innocents, including many Jews, who, after the war, were given British citizenship. Reading the House of Commons Hansard debate, 19th March 1990, I came across an amazing and enlightening statement by Lord Alex Carlile of Berriew, one of the most astute and highly respected legal thinkers of our time.

Lord Carlile was the lead prosecution barrister in a complex case I was involved in as a detective, which lasted six weeks at Chester Crown Court. I witnessed his great cross examination skills and keen legal mind. He later became an outstanding MP and went on to advise the British Government on anti-terror legislation in which he is a world renowned expert.

Lord Carlile spoke about his family who were murdered in Poland because they were Jews. His mother courageously escaped and this is what he told the House of Commons:

This year (1990), my mother will go to Poland for the first time in 45 years. She will bring herself to go to Poland following my father's death (he was never willing for her to go there) with me and with my sister who was born in Poland. She wishes to revisit some of the places which she knew as a child; but she will go with a heavy heart. She wishes to see those places again in her lifetime, but she will go against strains of memory as clear as crystal, and that will make it a difficult experience for her.

She and others can give evidence that would shame in quality some of the evidence given, for instance, last week in courts of law throughout Britain. She has described to me how, when she was fighting in the Warsaw uprising on a Warsaw street, she was stopped by two soldiers and she heard them discussing, in German, which she understood, but which they did not know she understood, whether she should be killed because she had an attractive leather bag. The Ukrainian soldier wished to murder her, but the German soldier thought that it would be wrong to murder her, so she was spared by the German soldier, who told her never to walk alone in a street in that city again.

She remembers that event as though it happened yesterday. She remembers what was in the bag, she remembers a description of the people who spoke to her, and the words that were used, even though they were spoken in a language that was not her own. My mother escaped from a ghetto in Lwow, now in the Ukraine. She escaped hidden in a hay cart. She remembers the details, and has described them to me, of how she came to escape, who helped her, the circumstances in which they helped her, the details and even the weather on the day she escaped.

I cannot begin to understand how the Honourable Member for Orpington can allege that people's memories of such events can be compared with the memory of some minor traffic accident.[i]

Lord Carlile was making the point very clearly that the memory of the victim is extremely important and its value should not be diminished because of time.

The memory of the bystander may not be so clear and may be tainted because they may feel embarrassment and guilt over not acting or speaking out. Some bystanders do provide material in the form of witnessing an event, or retelling a story, of the actions of a perpetrator, victim or even a rescuer. That testimony can be reliable if it does not leave the person making that report vulnerable to criticism. Millions of people either witnessed, or were aware of, the mass murders taking place around them, and, for many reasons, which are not for us to judge, did nothing at all to help. I will outline more in a later chapter.

There are also memories in the form of independent testimony by bystanders. There are very few of these testimonies, other than the reports found which the authorities made during the course of the war, which are unemotionally attached to the event. One such testimony is that of Kazimierz Sakowicz, a journalist who lived opposite anti-tank trenches in a village called Ponary just outside Vilnius in Lithuania.

Sakowicz recorded in his daily diary in matter of fact way the murder by shooting of between 50,000 Jewish men, women and children by Lithuanian and German police units opposite his home. This diary was found in various portions in bottles buried by Sakowicz and discovered after his death at the end of the war.[ii]

Then there is the memory of the rescuers. Many rescuers were humble and played down their heroic actions. Many rescuers were never spoken of again. The testimony to what they did comes from many survivors or those who witnessed the wonderful work they did. Yad Vashem, the Holocaust Memorial Centre in Jerusalem, recognises 25,685 rescuers or those who are aptly named "Righteous Among the Nations." This memory is very important and encourages us all that in the midst of tragic acts beyond imagination there were those who acted with courage and conviction.

One rescuer who displayed such humility was Dutch Protestant Pastor Evert Smelik. In 1978, as a result of testimony to show that he had rescued Jews, Yad Vashem honoured his actions by recognising him as "Righteous." Evert declined the honour by stating that he could have done more to help and rescue Jews. He wrote: 'Perhaps some of the saved with kind intentions, have exaggerated my slight interventions.[iii] Obviously there are memories by both rescuers and those rescued which come from different perspectives.

There are those who don't want to remember for various reasons. Many in Christendom choose to forget the Church's part in the Holocaust. Their memory is similar to those of the perpetrator or bystander and is very selective. We must be reminded of the events which really took place in the Holocaust, and what steered public opinion during the period prior to and during the genocide. What led to the murderous actions of people living in a Christian society?

When senior Church leaders today speak about Holocaust and enter the realm of repentance they speak about Christians in their congregations who were the perpetrators. An example of this is in Hungary, where before the Holocaust, Church leaders incited hatred by their antisemitic speeches. Pulpits were full of hatred towards Jews. In 1919 Ottokár Prohászka, the Bishop of Székesfehérvár wrote;

In our case it is important to note that the Jews are eating us up and we have to defend ourselves against this bedbug epidemic. It is absolutely true that there are good Jews, but Jewry is foreign, a foreign power that suppresses Christianity, conquers and exploits us ... Here we are dealing with the rampage of a cunning, faithless, and immoral race, a bedbug invasion, a rat campaign. There is only one question: How do we defend ourselves?[iv]

This vitriolic hatred against all Jews, except converts, continued throughout the period of the Holocaust.

During the 1944 deportations of Jews senior Church leaders remained silent and failed to direct their subordinates. Randolph Braham wrote in his book *The Christian Churches of Hungary and the Holocaust*; 'the failure of the top church leaders to take a public stand in defence of the Jews had a negative influence on most of the bishops and clergy at large. Their passive stance emboldened the Jews' enemies as much as it discouraged potential rescuers.'[v]

After the War Hungarian Church leaders spoke of repentance in terms of blaming their congregants. This is a further quote from Brahams book;

On the occasion of the fiftieth anniversary of the Holocaust in Hungary, the Hungarian Catholic Bishops' Conference and the Ecumenical Council of the Churches of Hungary (A Magyar Katolikus Püspöki Konferencia és a Magyarországi Egyházak Okumenikus Tanácsa) issued a joint declaration stating, among other things:

"[We] commemorate in piety the tragic events of fifty years ago, when Jews living in Hungary were dragged off to concentration camps and slaughtered in cold blood. We consider it as the greatest shame of our twentieth century that hundreds of thousands of lives were extinguished merely because of their origin…

"On the occasion of the anniversary we have to state that not only the perpetrators of this insane crime are responsible for it but all those who, although they declared themselves members of the churches, through fear, cowardice, or opportunism, failed to raise their voices against the mass humiliation, deportation, and murder of their Jewish neighbours. Before God we now ask forgiveness for this failure committed in the time of disaster fifty years ago."[vi]

There are records in the Vatican archives and hidden in the desks of Christian denominational leaders which tell the truth. We have no access to many of these documents at this time and therefore we are vulnerable to believing lies. Despite recent Popes speaking about repentance they have never attributed any blame to "The Church".

As a result few Christians today have any knowledge of Christian complicity in Holocaust. The Old Testament prophet Jeremiah speaks about such things: 'O LORD, my strength and my stronghold, my refuge in the day of trouble, to you shall the nations come from the ends of the earth and say: Our ancestors have inherited nothing but lies, worthless things in which there is no profit.' (Jeremiah 16:19).

My plea is that we should not be vulnerable to lies or those in Christendom who choose to forget. We must not let those who record our history, and who were complicit in The Holocaust, or have anti-Semitic sympathies, condemn Christians who do not want to repeat the past.

In short, "Christians" who incite hatred of Jews today must not succeed in seeing our generation continue the incitement of the past.

The Christian Church today is suffering from a 'convenient amnesia' which is dulling our feelings and emotions in regard to Holocaust and it leaves us vulnerable to those who would have us incite hatred towards Jews and Israel today. The reason for this amnesia will become clear as you read on.

The memory of the victim is extremely important and its value should not be diminished because of time.

Chapter 2 ~ What Do We Know About The Holocaust?

My congregation have held Holocaust exhibitions for 15 years and we have spoken to and questioned many attendees. We have also carried out surveys on the street, interviewing members of the public of all ages and backgrounds. When questioned about the Holocaust these are some of the things which spring to the minds of people: deaths of six million, Nazis, Germans, death camps, Auschwitz, Belsen, and the cattle truck trains transporting Jews.

Some didn't know that the six million deaths total applied to Jews. Some think a handful of Nazis murdered all six million Jews, or that all were murdered at Auschwitz. Some really have no idea how the Holocaust began or whether or not the perpetrators were brought to trial. Some of those who know that there was a trial at the end of the war, believe that all the perpetrators were brought to justice and executed.

So what about the 13 Nuremburg Trials between 1945 and 1949 held in the German city? They were aimed at bringing to justice some of those who were responsible for ordering the murders. These defendants were just a few of those who were responsible for Second World War crimes against humanity, particularly against Jews. The laws governing the trials were a mixture of American and British jurisdictions and led to the United Nations Genocide Convention of 1948, the Geneva Convention and the 1949 Laws and Customs of War. The trials, however, were not conclusive and certainly not a 'catch all.'

Many of the perpetrators, including Hitler, committed suicide. Many escaped justice. Only 24 senior Nazi officers appeared in court. Only 33 witnesses testified for the prosecution. Other smaller trials continued, but it took an individual, Simon Wiesenthal, and the foundation named after him, to trace and bring to justice some of the escapers. Only six Nazi organisations were indicted at the Nuremburg Trials. The international judges found 21 of the 24 defendants guilty, of whom 12 were sentenced to death. The remaining 12 were given prison sentences ranging from 12 years to life.

Journalists reporting on the trials described them as boring in the extreme. As cases lasted so long the public lost interest. People's desire to put the war behind them and look forward to a better future led to many war criminals not being prosecuted.

Today we have forgotten the fact that thousands of ordinary people rounded up Jews and shot them in forests or on the edges of anti-tank trenches and pits throughout German occupied territories. These shocking events happened in the centre of Christian communities throughout German occupied territories. Thousands of churchgoers committed brutal murders in their own towns and villages. Many were also involved in the process of mass murders the in the death camps. These ordinary people who had become vicious killers were never indicted or even investigated. Thousands of perpetrators returned to their homes and families and never spoke about their crimes as they escaped justice. They covered up their involvement by keeping silent and consequently were never held accountable or even considered for prosecution.

We don't remember, or don't even consider the fact, that police officers and ordinary men and women from varied backgrounds living in Nazi occupied countries were never brought to justice. Many of those who escaped were church attendees and in some cases clergy and theologians.

Some clergy championed genocide but were not considered for investigation or brought to account for their involvement in the atrocities. Other Christian leaders incited hatred against Jews. Some clergy, because of their sermons or silence, influenced many in their congregations to commit murder. Yitzhak Arad, in a paper published by Yad Vashem, entitled *The Christian Churches and the Persecution of Jews in the Occupied Territories of the U.S.S.R.,* states:

Even before the Einsatzgruppen, the special units of the SS, began the mass killing of Jews with the help of local auxiliaries, pogroms were carried out by the native population, killing thousands of Jews in Lvov, Kovno and many other localities in the Ukraine, Lithuania and Latvia. The heads of the churches in those areas were silent when their followers carried out these atrocities.[vii]

There is no real memory of these events because they have rarely been subject to scrutiny in post-war Christian communities. It is something sections of Christendom are desperate to forget. Arad continued:

A further indication of the Church's involvement was that Lithuanian chaplains served in some of these 'units of death.' The Lutheran Church in

Latvia and Estonia assumed a similar attitude. In these Baltic countries the ruling churches remained silent.[viii]

Since the war, Christian leaders who incited hatred against Jews or in some way encouraged those in their congregations to murder Jews, have remained silent about their complicity, or denied involvement, or have not even been accused. There are no voluntary testimonies from such clergy admitting their complicity. There are no voluntary statements from the pews disclosing their own criminal behaviour during the period in question. All we have are documents or statements which implicate those who were involved. Christian conspirators, or those Christians who incited the killing of innocent Jews, have remained silent or denied their actions.

Chapter 3 ~ Denial

There are eight stages to all genocides, denial being the final one. Denial is something Christendom has done throughout history with great skill and persuasion, not least regarding its involvement in the Holocaust. The following accounts gave me the incentive to remind today's Christians about the role the Church played in the Holocaust.

Many Christians today have no idea of what happened in the Holocaust; for others, it is a deliberate amnesia. There are, of course, valid and important recollections of those Christians who extended bravery beyond imagination and rescued Jews, often resulting in their brutal death and the deaths of their friends and relatives. However, the Church must not deny the fact that many within Christendom fuelled the Holocaust, and many Christians committed or were complicit in the atrocities.

Today many call for Governments and nations to repent over what happened in the Holocaust but they don't see the need for the Church to repent. I have taught the shocking truth in nations occupied by Germany during the Second World War. These countries include Belarus, Holland, Lithuania and also Germany itself.

I have found that churches either don't know about Christian anti-Semitism before or during the Holocaust or they blame the Roman Catholic Church alone for what happened. They deny their own denomination's responsibility. The fact is that Christians from every denomination were involved in the incitement against Jews and their mass execution.

Examples of denial are striking. Time between events allows for facts to be forgotten, distorted, ignored or denied. Holocaust denial, a phenomenon many find hard to understand, is a growing issue. Recently a Church of England priest was a speaker at an anti-Semitic conference in Iran during which he stood alongside Holocaust deniers. This gives credibility to denial particularly in countries such as Iran.

Another example of denial is in regard to a murder camp at Jasenovac in Croatia. Little is known about this camp in churches today, but thousands of Jews, Serbs and Gypsies were brutally killed there. The murder total is hotly disputed by Croats and Serbs. As the war was ending the camp was destroyed to hide the evidence of the brutal mass murder of men women and children. Heading the slaughter was an ordained Jesuit priest.

In 2012 Father Stjepan Razum, who obtained a PhD in Medieval Church history and who is the chairman of the Archbishopric Archive in Zagreb, Croatia, said that Jasenovac was just a "temporary labour camp" and that there was "no proof of mass executions."[ix] This is an example of Holocaust denial by an academic within the Church.

Whilst studying at Yad Vashem I was involved in the questioning of a Vatican representative regarding the October 1943 roundups of the Jews in Rome and their executions, and what the Roman Catholic Church and, in particular, the Pope knew about this. The accusation that Pope Pius X11 was silent was at the centre of this questioning. As a detective I was trained in interview techniques. What I remember very clearly was that this well-educated diplomat was adept at avoiding questions and denying some very clear evidence of the Pope remaining silent, despite knowing about the atrocities taking place.

My questions were about Cardinal Hlond of Poland, an anti-Semitic agitator who incited hatred against Jews. When I questioned the diplomat, rather than answer he remained silent. There have been numerous attempts, to no avail, for the Vatican to release papers concerning The Holocaust. The Roman Catholic Church also denies that many senior priests helped leading Nazis escape after the war. These include the Austrian Bishop, Alois Hudal. He established escape routes and safe places for fleeing senior Nazis to hide.

Deliberate memory suppression of what happened in the war is a form of denial. I visited Lithuania twice in 2015, once to teach about Israel and the Holocaust and once on a visit to Vilnius. I also visited museums and archivists. A Lithuanian historian was on the course I taught. What was interesting was that not only did I find a reluctance to speak about Christian complicity in the Holocaust, something which is evident from records and testimony in Lithuania, there was a real reluctance to speak about the role of the Church at the time. Another person on the course asked me not to teach about this subject as it could offend Roman Catholics taking the course.

I found there was little Holocaust educational material at Lithuanian museums and memorials. This is despite the fact that 95 per cent of Lithuanian Jewry, 195,000 souls, were massacred in three years, most between June and December 1941. However, there are Christians from Lithuania and other nations in Europe, albeit few in number, who have a real desire to bring things that have been hidden into the light, and I applaud them for that.

Edward Heath, one of Britain's Prime Ministers, said in a debate in Parliament on the subject of prosecution of War Criminals and referring to Holocaust Denial "There may be one or two maniacs who say that they never occurred, but who takes any notice of them? No one does so for a moment".[x] As we have read, it is not one or two maniacs who deny the truths of Holocaust it is organisations, Christian and non-Christian academics and those with an agenda to wipe away the memory.

Christian anti-Semitism has always involved Church denial of the facts. I have therefore made strenuous efforts here to quote eminent and accredited historians, those who have researched and written extensively about the subject. I have done so in an effort to give support for my claims that the Holocaust couldn't have taken place without Christianity, and that many Christians and leading theologians not only fuelled the Holocaust, but were actively complicit in the murder of millions of Jews, or were actual perpetrators.

As time has moved on, many find guilt harder to deal with or even accept, particularly in regard to the complicity of Christianity in the Holocaust. Speaking at a ladies' meeting, I stated that without Christendom the Nazi Holocaust couldn't have taken place. A lady immediately interjected: "I hope you substantiate that statement." "Of course," I said and I went on to prove my point. Her interruption, however, reflects the reluctance to hear about the Church's role in the Holocaust. Was her statement a denial of the possibility or a desire to forget?

Sadly, much has been hidden in Christendom. One reason for the reaction from that particular lady may be because of the faulty perception that all Christians were rescuers and could not be persecutors. There are many stories about Christian rescuers. We revel in what these courageous men and women did. While we have to remember the acts of these wonderful brave people, we must also consider all the horrific details of the Holocaust in an informed way.

Christian leaders and historians can use the example of Christian rescuers as a way of obfuscating the truth. Concealment of truth is often the reason why Christendom repeats the past and persecutes, abuses and misinforms congregations about Jews and Israel. Personal denial of our past is not an option and certainly not within Christendom, when repentance is a fundamental tenet of our faith.

I hope I have been able to clearly express my reasoning in exposing the truth. My hope and prayer is that Christians will not look back with rose tinted spectacles, just remembering those who were rescued, but that we will view the past with a repentant heart. We need to recognise what the Church did in conspiring with the killers and inciting ordinary people to hate Jews. We cannot continue to deny the Church's role and attribute the crimes to a few Nazis. Only when we realise the truth of Church incitement of hatred against the Jews can we turn away from hating Jews and Israel and begin to offer support.

Deliberate memory suppression of what happened in the war is a form of denial.

Chapter 4 ~ Christian Anti-Semitism

The question often asked is, how much more material should be written about anti-Semitism? The answer is simple: as long as anti-Semitism is expressed in society or in churches. We should oppose this hatred with all that we have and in as many ways as we can. Anti-Semitism's most obscene consequence is the Shoah or the Holocaust. We must not let anti-Semitism continue, remembering that in the past it has led to persecution and indescribable evil. We must continually flag up anti-Semitism's inherent danger.

There were 1,168 anti-Semitic attacks in the UK reported in 2014. The incitement to vilify Israel is taking ever more inventive forms and looks set to continue. Robert Wistrich entitled one of his many classic books on the subject *The Longest Hatred.* This aptly describes the unrelenting and insidious prejudice against a single people group in all history. Empires, kings, governments and religions have held on to this cruel, distorted attitude as if their very existence relied upon it. Sadly, it continues today in this so called modern and enlightened age. Christendom is also a constant in this hate story, with new and ever changing forms under the guise of anti-Zionism or anti-Israelism.

The Assyrians, Babylonians, Greeks and Romans all played a part in attempting to destroy the Jewish people and their religion, Judaism. But none achieved what Christianity has accomplished in its 2,000-year crusade against the Jews. Christianity has never achieved a total annihilation of Jewish communities but so far it has been the most virulent anti-Semitic organisation in history. The attitude flourishes today even as Islamic terror groups take root in the Middle East and have already slaughtered most of the region's remaining Christians.

I want to make it clear that I am a Bible-believing Christian. My belief in justice is why I want to elicit from the darkest corners Christendom's best kept secret sins. Things done or said in Christendom which had a significant role in the Holocaust are rooted in Church history. Anti-Semitic attitudes and vitriolic rhetoric rumbling on into the 1930s caused ordinary Christian families to hate their Jewish neighbours and become their betrayers and murderers under Nazi rule.

Please note that it was without doubt Church leaders who poisoned the minds of ordinary folk in Austria, Germany and other European nations. This allowed Hitler to have full support for his plan to wipe Jewry out of Europe. In short, Christian leaders prepared and incited followers to fulfil Hitler's evil dream of a Europe free of God's Chosen People.

After Christianity took on a Gentile leadership, the Jewish roots of the faith were discarded. Franklyn H Littell, the respected Christian historian and theologian, explained to me that this process was a victory of paganism over the Church and "bad for the Jews." The apostle Paul, in Romans 11:18, tells us that the Jewish root supports our faith. Yet Christendom tore out this root from the foundations of our faith and absorbed paganism. The Church turned against the very people and religion on which our faith is built.

My concern is that Christendom doesn't know its anti-Semitic history. Churches have not taught about the evil acts of the past. We would rather not know about eras when, in the name of Jesus, Jewish communities were destroyed, and, if we did want to know, much of what was done has been hidden from us. However, the further in the past the event, the more likely we are to accept that there was then strong anti-Semitism.

Much has been written about the Early Church. As we look at the gap in time since the first centuries of Christianity, and its hateful attitudes towards Jews, we are prone to reflect that this anti-Semitism was a long time ago.

We content ourselves by saying that we are now more civilised and understanding, but those early century sermons, writings and attitudes were the seeds of anti-Semitism that flourished throughout the Christian era. The Church has allowed these heresies to grow into a twisted, thorny tree that has borne the fruit of murder and the destruction of Jewish communities by Christians who believed they were doing God's will.

The Holocaust-Shoah is the result of the worst example of anti-Semitism, but sadly not the only example. Christian anti-Zionism has morphed into the current harvest of anti-Semitism. We have leaders with large followings who speak at Christian and non-Christian conferences all over the world. They vilify Israel and lie about what is happening in the Jewish state. Israel is accused of being an occupying, oppressive regime. The director of one of the largest Christian charities, Embrace Middle East, supports the Muslim Brotherhood and blames Israel for the plight of

Coptic Christians in Egypt.

Their stances are misleading, illogical and rooted in anti-Semitism, yet some of these leaders are highly regarded within Christendom. Christian organisations such as the Amos Trust, Sabeel and the Kairos group all portray Israel as aggressors, when the truth is that they are defending their population from enemies who want to completely annihilate them. Why would Christian groups today want to support those with a genocidal vision? As you will read there are similarities in the way Christian leaders in the years prior and during Holocaust supported the Nazi ideology and in fact were members of the Nazi party.

My purpose is to remind people what it was like in Europe before and during the Holocaust. Statements by Christian leaders fomented such hatred that they resulted in ordinary churchgoers ending up as mass killers because they believed what was said in the pulpit. Teaching in Germany, I was struck by the sincere desire of many Christians not simply to repent of what happened under the Nazis, but to find out what actually happened and by whom, even to investigating the involvement of their own families. This real desire was to endeavour to ensure that such atrocities could not happen again in their country.

I cannot tell you how much I admire and respect what many Christians in Germany are doing. This will be of tremendous value for Germany's future and is pleasing to God.

However, for most within Christendom I see a culture of blame. Governments and community leaders are accused of Holocaust atrocities but there is a culture of denial about Christendom being a co-driver of genocide. Most Holocaust historians say that without Christendom the Shoah could not have taken place, yet most Christian leaders do not acknowledge Church guilt and responsibility at all. There is much evidence to substantiate the historians' understanding, but Christendom in general ignores the facts. Nazis are cited by the Church as being the sole players in this terrible event. Clergy's top echelons simply refuse to accept Christendom's responsibility in promulgating pre-war fear and hatred of Jews. This has enabled the cover up regarding the murder of millions just because they, or their parents or grandparents, were Jews.

This immoral madness was rife amongst Christian communities in Europe. It was a cancerous tumour on an otherwise healthy body. This anti-Semitic tumour spread throughout Christian Europe, even though most adherents had high Christian values which would never usually or remotely end in acts of murder or encourage such a crime. Not acting when murders were taking place would, in normal circumstances, have been alien to their Christian understanding.

Their actions during the Holocaust in not acting to prevent the murders, or becoming murderers themselves, were a direct result of pulpit teaching which in their minds turned evil into good, and moral Christian standards were twisted into the diabolical idea that Jews were a danger to the world. This iniquity manifested itself to such an extent that Christians in Nazi occupied countries became willing murderers and conspirators in the rounding up of Jews to be shot or transported to the death camps.

Writing about The Holocaust, Dr. Eva Fogelman explained in her book *Conscience and Courage*:

"It was a reign which, nearly half a century later, still challenges our understanding. Evil was rewarded and good acts were punished. Bullies were aggrandized and the meek trampled. In this mad world, most people lost their bearings. Fear disoriented them, and self-protection blinded them."[xi]

Silence is a sign of support to those committing the crimes.

Chapter 5 ~ The Dehumanisation Process

What were the circumstances which turned ordinary men and women into killers? To answer that question we must look at the generation before the Holocaust to understand what formed the resolve of their offspring to commit mass murder with such zeal.

Was it only secular Germans who planned the elimination of the Jews, just a relatively small group? The Nazis were, of course, guilty but they were not the only participants. Christians from Nazi occupied Austria, Poland, Romania, Belorussia, Latvia, Lithuania, Romania, Netherlands, Belgium, France, Greece and Arab lands all played a part. Some nations had a small part, others a leading role in the Final Solution.

It wasn't just those with a Nazi ideology who brutally murdered innocent Jews. Ordinary people who were not members of the Nazi party, and who didn't vote for Hitler, joined the killing machine. Doctors, nurses, policemen, educators, shopkeepers, office workers, factory workers, public transport workers, lawyers, scientists and clergy from many nations played a role in murdering Jews. What led that generation, who were socially aware, intellectual, modern and respectable, to murder a minority group on an industrial scale and why did they do so when there was no moral, military or political reason?

To answer these questions we must accept that it is clear from the vast amount of evidence that Christian leaders set the agenda for elimination of Jews. Hitler and his accomplices just dictated the timing and method of this terrible genocide. Meanwhile many Church leaders incited such hatred that ordinary people, many of whom regularly attended church and professed a Christian faith, helped to carry out the slaughter.

After Hitler came to power in 1933, Nazi propaganda added to the belief that the Jews in Europe were enemies of the state and Church. Jews were perceived to be leading a Bolshevik revolution against Germany and the Church. A great deal has been written about Hitler's propaganda machine and how many European minds were indoctrinated. The truth is that Christian leaders sowed the seeds of hatred in the years prior to Hitler's rise to power. A staggering 95% of Germans had church affiliation. What they were taught in the pew enabled Hitler simply to turn the key to mass murder.

Christian leaders in a number of nations had dehumanised the Jew in the minds of their followers and unwittingly prepared the way for Hitler, with all his dark charisma and political authority, to give ordinary people permission to manifest the evil already planted in their hearts. Churches in many parts of Europe were awash with anti-Semitism, and the Nazi regime simply opened the door for it to burst out, causing a tidal wave of innocent Jewish blood wherever Austrian/German fascism ruled.

To kill in the manner and to the extent seen in The Holocaust there had to be a process of dehumanising of the Jews. The definition of dehumanising is 'to deprive someone of positive human qualities.' Without this element genocide cannot take place. In the minds of the perpetrator the victim has to be sub-human. The dehumanisation of Jews by Christendom goes far back in history and was rife when Hitler came to power. The process then manifested into a genocide we now call the Holocaust or Shoah.

Without doubt what many leaders in Christendom did and said during the years leading up to and during the Holocaust practically brainwashed worshippers from Roman Catholic and Protestant churches to act in the most callous and murderous ways imaginable. The Holocaust was not a frenzied unplanned attack, it was carefully considered and orderly. The murders not only involved many of the eight million Nazi party members but also ordinary members of society, and many Christian leaders and their followers, who had little or no leaning towards politics or the Nazi party.

I emphasise, however, that there were Christians and clergy who were executed because they assisted Jews. Yad Vashem, the Jerusalem Holocaust Memorial, has honoured many Roman Catholic leaders as "Righteous among the Nations," particularly Polish priests. However, they were a minority and not a true reflection of Christendom during the war. Avraham Tory in his book "Surviving the Holocaust" shows his indebtedness to the Roman Catholic priest Bronius Paukstys who rescued him and many others from the Kovno Ghetto in Lithuania. We must not forget clergy and Christians from every denomination who were executed as result of attempting to save Jews.

However, my purpose here is to focus on those who incited hatred and either condoned or encouraged the murder of Jews. Every denomination in Christendom, in every nation in Europe, led the way in this process of incitement and conspiracy. We must all understand that we cannot ignore Christianity's culpability in the Holocaust.

To return to the question as to how the generation who took part in genocide came to believe that Jews were sub-human we must examine how their thoughts and attitudes were influenced and by whom. A good starting point is what was said by Church leaders to the parents of the perpetrators. In August 1871 Pope Pius IX made it clear to a female gathering how they should feel about the Jews of Rome. He said:

Before the time of Jesus, Jews had been the children of God but all this had changed owing to their obstinacy and their failure to believe. We have in Rome today these people everywhere, there are too many of these dogs. We hear them barking in the streets going about molesting people everywhere.[xii]

These women, I am sure, would have been from influential families or they would not have been granted an audience with the Pope. They naturally would have shared what they had heard from someone they espoused as one of great spiritual leaders of the day, the Pope, with friends, families and their peers. I am sure that the Pope didn't just influence this group but through them he must have influenced everyone they would have later come in contact with.

These women were the grandmothers and mothers of the generation who committed the very act of genocide. My own mother believed everything the Pope said, or for that matter the priests said, so I am aware how someone in authority can affect how ordinary people think. There is no doubt that the Pope's statement incited anti-Semitism to the women who naturally would have passed on his views to family and friends.

In 1880 Roman Catholic Church publications sided with the sentiments of the Russian pogroms, which resulted in the massacres of many Jewish communities, by vilifying Jewish literature. These publications fuelled anti-Semitism, not just endorsed it.

Planted in readers' minds was the idea that Jews were responsible for many aspects of social inequality and poverty. The Jesuit bi-weekly *Civilita Cattolica*, founded in 1850, influenced politics as well as the thoughts of its readers. Articles instilled fear and a need for protection against Jews, in short making Jews enemies of Catholics and governments.

One edition said in 1880:

Jews were obligated by their religion to hate non-Jews and as a consequence Christians despised them. Societies have to protect themselves from the Jews, and governments would be well advised to introduce exceptional laws for a race that is so exceptionally and profoundly perverse.[xiii]

In another article the bi-weekly said:

As history has shown, if this foreign Jewish race is left too free, it immediately becomes the persecutor, oppressor, tyrant, thief and devastator of the country in which it lives. Special laws must be introduced to keep Jews in their place.[xiv]

In 1920 the publication called Jews 'the filthy element who were avid for money.'[xv] Father Oreglia, a writer for the newspaper, compared 'Jews to wolves and that they should not be set free.'[xvi]

Imagine the consequences such statements would have on the readers of this well respected publication. The parents of Holocaust perpetrators would have been taken in by these articles which were written by priests with the clear intention of dehumanising Jews. The idea of restrictions on Jews and their freedoms was not a new idea to Europe during Hitler's rule. Hitler's mother, raised in anti-Semitic Roman Catholic Austria, had been exposed to these perverse opinions when Hitler was growing up.

Many Catholic and Protestant clergymen spoke and wrote articles agreeing with the forgery *The Protocols of the Elders of Zion*, concocted by the Okhrana, the Tsar's secret police, around the beginning of the 20th Century. The book opined that Jews had a plan to rule the world.[xvii]

In 1920 Monsignor Jouin, supporting it, wrote: 'From a triple viewpoint of race, nationality and religion, the Jew has become the enemy of humanity.'[xviii] Jouin was later congratulated for his views by Cardinal Gasparri of Rome.

Susan Zuccotti in her book *The Italians and The Holocaust*, highlights the anti-Semitic vigour in which renegade priest Giovanni Preziosi translated and promoted the fraudulent protocols book. Preziosi moved to Germany in July 1943 and met Hitler. He wrote six articles for the official Nazi newspaper *Volkischer Beobachtera* which gave credibility to *The Protocols of the Elders of Zion* and supported its lies. He also made radio broadcasts vilifying Jews in the hope of influencing Italian listeners. [xix]

In the 1920s Father Enrico Rosa, a veteran journalist described as the 'intrepid champion of the directives of the Holy See,' wrote:

The Jews were to blame for the Russian Revolution as they had been for the French Revolution and as they have been for the most recent one in Hungary, with all of its massacres, cruelty and savage horrors. The result has been the collapse of the Muscovite Empire and the tyranny imposed by the Bolshevik takeover which remains in Europe.[xx]

In 1922 *Civilta Cattolica* published an article from their Austrian correspondent which said that if Jews had their way in Austria

Vienna will be nothing but a Judaic city; property and houses will all be theirs. The Jews will be the bosses and the gentlemen and the Christians their servants..... Austria will be absolutely the subject, tributary and slave to the Jews or it will not exist at all.[xxi]

At the end of the 19th century the Vatican daily L'*Osservatore Romano*, said to reflect the views of the Holy See, published an article which said:

Anti-Semitism ought to be the natural, sober, thoughtful Christian reaction against Jewish predominance ... True anti-Semitism is and can be in substance nothing other than Christianity, completed and perfected in Catholicism.[xxii] These publications directly affected the generation in question and promoted hatred so great that the act of murder of Jews became not only a possibility but a reality.

In 1937 *L'Osservatore Romano*, promoted the idea that Jews were 'a foreign body that irritates and provokes the reaction of the organism it has contaminated.'[xxiii] In the same year the publication reviewed a book by the well regarded Anglo-French writer and historian Hilaire Belloc, a Catholic ant-Semite. It echoed Belloc's view that the Jewish problem could only be solved by 'elimination or by segregation.[xxiv] During the war, when the mass killing of Jews by shooting and gassing took place, the newspaper continued to fuel hatred by publishing articles accusing Jews of ritual murder and of being Christ killers.

On the eve of Kristallnacht, Civilta Cattolica accused Jews of being a danger to the world. Kristallnacht, a pre-planned attack on the Jews of East Prussia, Austria and Germany on 9th and 10th November 1938, resulted in 1,000 synagogues being destroyed, and 7,500 Jewish businesses ransacked. Jewish hospitals, schools and libraries were also damaged. At least 91 Jews were killed and 30,000 imprisoned. The article by the Roman Catholic press would, without doubt, have been written with Nazi collaboration to fuel hatred of Jews. The article stated:

The Jewish question will remain unsolved because, as all agree, even those most kindly disposed to the Jews and their corrupt Messianism, it's their fatal craving for worldwide financial and political domination that is the true cause that makes Judaism a front of disorders and a permanent danger for the world.[xxv]

The truth is that Christian leaders sowed the seeds of hatred in the years prior to Hitler's rise to power.

Chapter 6 ~ Church and State

What religious leaders say has a huge effect on society. We see that today in Islam, particularly in the Middle East, when imams join forces with political leaders and foment hatred against Jews by making statements such as, 'Israel is an occupying force who stole Arab land.' These lies result in the daily tragedy we see on the streets of Israel. Crimes are committed by Palestinian Arab children as young as 11 years of age. Youngsters have stabbed Jews with knives provided by their parents.

Kristallnacht occurred in November 1938 and was planned to violate Jewish communities in Germany and Austria. This happened with devastating consequences for the Jewish communities. Everyone either witnessed or heard or read about the murders, arrests and destruction of Jewish property.

The following day in the German city of Nuremburg 100,000 attended an anti-Semitic rally. That was a huge number of people in one place for one purpose. We must therefore ask - was Kristallnacht a well-designed plan by politicians only or was Christendom a conspirator in what turned out to be a watershed in the way Jews were treated in Germany and Austria?

It was at Nuremburg in 1935 that laws were passed which deprived Jews of their rights. These laws were not new. They contained laws which Christendom had enacted against the Jews throughout history. Church councils, in the few years prior to The Holocaust, agreed with Hitler's racist agenda. The restrictions on Jewish life, including the yellow star, were all originally Christian initiatives. Hitler, without doubt, understood that the laws enacted against Jews would not be opposed by Christendom because churches had called for them to be enacted.

Anti-Semitic articles in Christian publications, in one form or another, were a daily occurrence in Austria and Germany in the years well before the Holocaust. These certainly would have influenced Hitler and certainly his mother, a devout Catholic. These publications would without doubt have a lasting effect on the attitudes of ordinary Germans and Austrians as they grew up to be the people of persecution.

Bible scholar Paul Anton De Lagarde, who died in 1891 and who Hitler much admired, was one of the founding fathers of Germany's pre-war anti-Semitism. Lagarde advocated a national form of Christianity, purged of any elements of Judaism or Jewish references. He said Jews should be destroyed as speedily as possible, as they were nothing more than pests and parasites.

This was not a new idea. Apostate Christendom, from its early years, had attempted to eradicate Judaism and Jews from Christian communities. The heretic Marcion in the second century removed the Tanach (Hebrew Scriptures), all references to John the Baptist and the genealogy of Yeshua (Jesus) to remove the fact that Yeshua was a Jew. Those who followed Marcion vilified Jews as the Devil's advocates and a scourge to society. Those sympathetic to Judaism within Christendom were executed as Judaisers. Keeping the fourth commandment (Saturday Sabbath) was punishable by death. Later on, communities throughout Europe that kept the traditional Sabbath or Passover were killed at the behest of Church leaders.

In AD 381, Pope Damasus took on the role of Babylonian priest. He paganised Roman Catholicism and created a regime which thrived on driving from its ranks any reference to Jews and their faith, which in reality Christianity was based on. The Vatican has never denounced Damasus's occult role, which has influenced Catholics throughout the centuries. Cardinal John Henry Newman said in the late 19th century that 69% of Catholic practice was derived from the pagans.[xxvi]

Martin Luther, the German theologian who led the Reformation, said that he hated the books of Esther and Maccabees because they contained too much Judaism. Shortly before his death Luther made a scathing attack on Jews in his book *The Jews and Their Lies*. Luther's anti-Semitism influenced German Protestants through to the 20th century. His instructions for Christians to burn Jewish books and synagogues led to extreme persecution of Jews in the 16th century.[xxvii] Luther's rants against Jews heavily influenced Protestant leaders who became key players in the mass murder of Jews under Nazi rule. Throughout the 1930s and during the Holocaust many Protestant clergy quoted Luther's anti-Semitic views with pride in their literature and sermons.

Karl Lueger, who died in 1910 in Austria, was a former Mayor of Vienna and leader of the Austrian Christian Social Party. Hitler greatly admired Lueger, regarding him as the 'greatest Burgermeister of all time.'[xxviii] In

1887 Lueger made a strong anti-Semitic speech in which he supported a government Bill aimed at preventing the immigration of Jews fleeing pogroms in Russia and Romania. In 1893 he was instrumental in bringing together various Christian factions into one group which became the Christian Social Party. Active within that party were outspoken anti-Semitic priests such as Father Deckert and Joseph Scheicher. Both had a great influence on their followers. The Christian Social Party often called for boycotts on Jewish businesses and had a direct influence on the younger generation by planting ideas of anti-Semitism which later enabled the Holocaust.

Bishop Alois Hudal, an Austrian Catholic who died in May 1963, was in the 1920s, fearless about what he said were the dangers of Austria's 220,000 Jews. Hudal said 'Nazi radicalism was equal to Christian teaching' and he affirmed Hitler's views. After the war, Hudal was actively involved in helping Nazi war criminals to escape justice through what we now term as the 'rat lines.' In the book *Unholy Trinity* by Mark Aarons and John Loftus, Hudal is described as the first priest after the war to rescue and support Nazi war criminals.[xxix]

The book describes how Hudal helped Franz Stangl, the commandant of the Treblinka camp that exterminated 900,000 people, mainly Jews, to make a new life in Syria. Stangl later described how Hudal gave him a passport and entrance visa to Syria and arranged work for him in Damascus. The Catholic relief agency Caritas also helped in the rat lines. The Wiesenthal organisation has evidence that Caritas paid for all of Eichmann's expenses to reach South America. Hudal organised the journey.

The world accuses Germans of being the sole perpetrators of the Holocaust but don't forget that over half the perpetrators of the crimes against Jews were led by Austrians, even Hitler was Austrian by birth. We must also remind ourselves that those such as Hudal were influential Catholic leaders, and it was they and their predecessors who dehumanised Jews in the minds of the Holocaust generation. This generation saw Jews, as the earlier Christian publications had done, as sub-human. The grouping included Hitler and his German and Austrian associates. This common hatred of Jews, which had its roots in apostate Christianity, enabled Hitler and his followers to proclaim that the elimination of Jews was imperative. The pre-war generation, who had been brainwashed by their parents and clergy, simply required Hitler's permission to become the perpetrators in the Holocaust, although not the only perpetrators.

On 20th July 1933, knowing the restrictions being placed upon Jews, Cardinal Eugenio Pacelli, a Vatican diplomat to Germany who became Pope during the war, signed an agreement with the Nazi party. The pact contained promises of Roman Catholic support for the Reich in return for rights for the Roman Catholic Church in Germany.

The Reich failed to keep many of its promises, but the Roman Church held to its agreement. During Pacilli's reign as Pope Pius XII he never criticised the Nazi party for the atrocities the Jews of Europe were experiencing and which he clearly knew were taking place. His defenders today say that a 1942 speech which he made at Christmas was an outspoken condemnation of the murder of the Jews.

Millions of Jews had already been gassed or shot in the Soviet Union, Poland, Lithuania, Latvia, Estonia, Romania, Serbia, Slovakia, Germany and Austria when Pope Pius XII stated:

We owe it to the innumerable dead ... to the suffering groups of mothers, widows and orphans ... to the innumerable exiles ... to the hundreds of thousands who, without personal guilt, are doomed to death or to a progressive deterioration of their condition, sometimes for no other reason than their nationality or descent ... to the many thousands of non-combatants whom the air war has harmed.[xxx]

I don't see any condemnation of the mass murders of Jews in this statement. In some ways had he made a critical assessment of what was happening it would have been hypocrisy?

In his book *Hitler and the Holocaust*, Robert Wistrich describes how, after the signing of the Concordat by Pacelli, thousands of Catholics flocked to the Nazi party in 1933. Wistrich also wrote about the Roman Catholic Archbishop of Munich, Michael Von Faulhaber, who preached a series of sermons defending the Hebrew Bible and the Jewish origins of Christianity. However, Faulhaber insisted that 'the indispensability of the Old Testament had no bearing on the antagonism to the Jews of the day which he did not seek to oppose.'[xxxi]

In her book *A Convenient Hatred*, Phyllys Goldstein tells the story of Edith Stein, (1891-1942) a Jew who converted to Catholicism in 1922 and became a respected Catholic educator. Edith wrote to the Pope Pius XI in

April 1933 stating:

Everything that happened in Germany, and continues to happen on a daily basis, originates with a government that calls itself Christian. For weeks, not only Jews but also thousands of faithful Catholics in Germany, and, I believe, all over the world, have been waiting and hoping for the Church of Christ to raise its voice to put a stop to this abuse of Christ's name.

Is not this idolisation of race and government power which is being pounded into the public consciousness by the radio open heresy? Is this not all diametrically opposed to the conduct of our Lord and Saviour, who, even on the cross, still prayed for His persecutors. [xxxii]

Pope Pius XI pontiff from 1922-1939 ignored her pleas. Her letters were never acknowledged. Edith, whose grandparents were Jewish, was murdered by the Nazis because of her ancestry. By the end of 1942 the Pope had been made aware of the Nazi atrocities taking place.

I teach a course throughout Europe about the Church's dealings with Jews. In the module on the Holocaust, I cite the heroic acts of SS Colonel Kurt Gerstein. From August 1942 he attempted to make the world and the Church aware of the mass murders taking place in Sobibor, Belzec and Treblinka. Kurt Gerstein attempted to meet with Monsignor Orsinego, the Papal Nuncio of Berlin, but he was denied an audience. He then made a report to the office of the Archbishop of Berlin, Cardinal Count Preysing, requesting that his report be forwarded to the Vatican. The Vatican has never denied that Gerstein's report was sent.

In her book *Italians and the Holocaust*, Susan Zuccotti makes the point that the Pope had been sent reports from his diplomatic representatives from several nations, and from leaders of Jewish organisations, about the atrocities as early as September 1942, but he failed to speak out. Zuccotti writes about the roundup of Italian Jews on 16th October 1943. She states that:

Had the Pope spoken out either publicly or privately through the goodwill of thousands of priests, he might have sounded an alarm and saved thousands of lives. He of all people would have been believed[xxxiii].

She adds: "Pope Pius XII did not just fail to speak out or exert private pressure before October 16th (referring to the roundup of Italian Jews in October 1943 which the Pope knew meant extermination) he also failed to issue a public protest after the roundup had actually occurred".

The Bible commands us to love our neighbours as ourselves. Christendom is obliged to teach that principle, given to us in the Jewish scriptures and repeated by Jesus Christ. Yet the Pope, and those around him, ignored the plight of 1,259 Jews, including 896 women and children, who on 16th October 1943 were being held in the military college only 600 feet away from Vatican City. These Jews were under guard awaiting trains to take them to the death camps. The Pope knew that the transportation by the SS of the Italian Jews meant their certain death. He knew about the shootings of thousands of Jews in Lithuania, Ukraine, Poland, Romania, Hungary and other Catholic countries. He knew about the gassing of Jews in the death camps. There was no outward sign of concern for those Jews situated outside the Pope's front door. Not speaking out against those who commit atrocities can be a sign of agreement. Being a bystander is not an option for the so-called "Vicar of Christ" or any Christian leader. Silence is a sign of support to those committing the crimes.

Martin Luther King said 'In the end, we remember not the words of our enemies but the silence of our friends.' [xxxiv] I find it sad that the most powerful religious leader in all of the occupied lands is remembered for his silence amid the screams of the suffering of those who Jesus calls members of His family in Mathew 25 v 40.

Chapter 7 ~ Complicity to Murder

Holocaust survivors' testimonies, published in Jan Grabowski's book *Hunt for the Jews*, reveals that Roman Catholic priests in Poland were complicit in the murder of Jews. Grabowski makes the point very concisely that Catholics were already primed to kill. He wrote: 'The growing radicalisation of anti-Jewish attitudes was, no doubt, directly linked to the campaign of hate during the 1930s led by the Catholic press.'[xxxv]

These anti-Semitic attitudes instilling hate made the life of ordinary Jews, living in Poland before the war, painful. Easter and Christmas were times during which Christians abused their Jewish neighbours. Grabowski's book quotes survivors such as Abraham Mahler, who claimed that one of the most active anti-Semites was the local priest. The book quotes a Polish philosopher, writing about the thoughts of Jews during the war, which is a chilling indictment of the Church:

The priest stands at the doorstep of the church and watches the carnival of death. This behaviour is untouched by Christianity, at the core you can see the pagan past. Indeed, in Poland, there is no concept of sin, because morality and faith have been pushed into the church, into that narrow shielded space inside the temple. There, you have to be good, righteous and clean. Once you step outside the church however, everything is allowed, and you can forget about your faith. God does not exist in the social, moral and intellectual sphere.[xxxvi]

In the absence of an official instruction from the Vatican regarding the Jewish persecution, Grabowski writes that clergy had to decide for themselves what they should do: 'Some, such as the priest from Radomsyl Wielki, first incited peasants against Jews and later refused to return the Jewish items which they had previously been entrusted with.'[xxxvii] Polish priests were influenced by what Grabowski describes as 'the growing radicalisation of anti-Jewish attitudes was no doubt, directly linked to the campaign of hate led, during the 1930s, by the Catholic press.'[xxxviii]

There is ample evidence of collaboration between clergy and the murderers. One Waffen SS report dated 12th August 1941 referred to the mass killing of Jews - men, women and children, in the Pripet marshes of the Ukraine. It states: 'Ukrainian clergy were very co-operative and made themselves available for every action.'[xxxix] An action describes the period between the detention and murder of Jews.

Chapter 8 ~ Church Leaders Beyond Europe

Church leaders in the UK and America also knew about the murder of Jews. In January 1942 the British Ambassador to the Vatican, Sir Francis d'Arcy Osborne, was well aware of Hitler's speech about the liquidation of the Jews. The following July, Osborne was critical of the Vatican's silence about the murder of over a million Jews by that time, including 700,000 Polish Jews. In October 1942 Father Pirro Scavizzi informed the Vatican with evidence of the murder of two million Jews. There is no defence to the charge that Christian leaders, not only in the occupied lands but throughout Europe and America, were well aware and fully briefed about the atrocities taking place during the war.

Walter Laqueur's book *The Terrible Secret* provides evidence that In March 1942 three senior leaders of the Jewish community in Europe met Monsignor Bernardini, the Papal Nuncio in Switzerland, and handed him a detailed report about the mass killings of Jews. Bernardini stated that he was aware of the situation and had previously informed the Vatican but would make this new report known to Rome.[xl] The racial cleansing of Polish Jews was made known to the world by June 1942.

In June and July 1942, Cardinal Hinsley, the Archbishop of Westminster, reported on radio that he was aware of the mass shootings of Jews in Poland. R. Lichtheim, the head of the Zionist Movement in Geneva, made it clear to UK politicians, who debated in Parliament the issue of Jewish resettlement, that deportation meant death to the Jews.

Jewish leaders in the UK and the US provided numerous reports of what was happening, but even before the Holocaust started, Church leaders in the UK and the US protested but these protestations did not have the support of their congregations or their Governments and Politicians. Victoria Barnett wrote in her paper *The Role of the Churches - Compliance and Confrontation*:

Between 1933 and 1945, there were six major statements from the leaders of Churches in this country and in Europe (outside the Third Reich) that specifically condemned anti-Semitism and the Nazi persecution of Jews. (Among the officials involved were the Archbishop of Canterbury and

Samuel Cavert and Henry Smith Leiper of the Federal Council of Churches in New York.)

In November 1938, the three leading Protestant ecumenical organizations in Geneva, Switzerland, issued a statement castigating "antisemitism in all its forms" and urging governments to permit more Jewish refugees to enter their countries. In the United States in December 1938, the Federal Council of Churches and the U.S. Catholic bishops issued a joint condemnation of Kristallnacht, which had occurred a month earlier. (It was the first Protestant/Catholic joint statement on a social issue in this country.) In December 1942, after reports of genocide began to reach the Allied countries, the Federal Council of Churches passed a resolution protesting the "virtual massacre" of Europe's Jews.

This was followed by similar protests from the Anglican Church in England and a joint statement by Protestant ecumenical leaders and the World Jewish Congress in Geneva. In Great Britain, the Archbishop of Canterbury, William Temple, gave an impassioned speech in March 1943 in the House of Lords, demanding an immediate end to immigration quotas and an increase in Allied aid to countries that offered refuge to Jews. In a 1983 speech delivered at Hebrew Union College in Cincinnati, Gerhardt Riegner, the director of the World Jewish Congress in Geneva during the war (and a man who had participated in efforts to rescue Jews from the Nazis), said that, during the Holocaust, "the human understanding, friendship, and the helping hand" of his Protestant ecumenical colleagues "were the only signs of the light in the darkness that surrounded us"

These aspects of the Christian Churches' opposition to the Third Reich did not, of course, impede the workings of the Holocaust, or even lead to the rescue of significant numbers of endangered Jews. The actions and pronouncements described here were not part of any long-term, comprehensive and coordinated program. The Christian leaders outside of Germany who spoke out against the persecution of the Jews and against genocide were a minority in the Christian world. They failed to win significant support from their own Church members."[xli]

The lack of support for those Church leaders who shouted out may be due to a number of reasons, not least anti-Semitic Clergy who had massive followings. In America, Catholic Priest Father Charles Coughlin was the most famous. Coughlin (1891-1978) had a huge following. It was said

34

that he had more mail than Roosevelt. In his home village they opened up a Post Office to cope with his mail, said to be 80,000 per week. Roosevelt who could never be considered Pro-Jew used Coughlin in his election campaign.

In 1926 Coughlin, who was fully supported by his Bishop, broadcast his first of a regular Sunday show live on radio. Coughlin demonised the Jews of America and Europe, spreading the idea that they were a dangerous Bolshevist enemy of the World. Even after Kristallnacht in November 1938 Coughlin promoted the Nazi state's violent actions against Jews stating that it was retaliation for Jewish persecution of Jews.

Listening to this anti-Semite, in many films there are of his speeches during this time, turns my stomach. Not because one man had such hate in his heart for Jews who had blessed America and Europe, but because millions of people applauded him and gave him financial support. Thus when American Clergy, who without such massive support, spoke out against the atrocities in Europe they were ignored.

In the UK there was a rather more discreet anti-Semitism, with the exception of Oswald Mosley's Fascist Party. Politicians were less outspoken, as were clergy, and chose in the majority of cases to remain silent. We do know that in 1937 Churchill said that Jews were partly to blame for their own persecution, though we could never say he was anti-Semitic.[xlii]

However, in light of the lack of support for Jews trying desperately to leave Europe before the War and after the war trying to make their way to Israel there had to be both political and religious influential voices who, behind the scenes, held strong views against Jews. Had there been the political and Christian support for the Archbishop of Canterbury's impassioned plea to the House of Lord's in 1943 the Government may have focused a little more on helping the already desperate and decimated Jews of Europe.

Prior to and during The Holocaust, Christian leaders maintained the heretical and dangerous verbal abuse of Jews and Judaism which resulted in their brutal genocide. An example of this can be found in the records of debates in Parliament about Jews during Holocaust. I am currently reading through Hansard (the record of Parliamentary debates) for the period of the War. On 19th May 1943 Sir Austen Hudson MP for Hackney North made the following statement during a debate on "The Refugee Problem"

At that time it was known by MP's that 2 million Jews had already been murdered.

"I would like to say a word about anti-Semitism. I know something about this subject, in view of the peculiar composition of my own constituency. I am aware that there is ill-feeling between the Jews and the Christians in my constituency. There is no doubt about that. But I am convinced that that ill-feeling is not political in any way. It arises from the fact that in the last decade or so, large numbers of people, who have only recently come from the Continent, have come to live in that neighbourhood.

Their customs, their ways of living, are different. I know, from the letters I have received, asking whether it is true that many more aliens are coming, that some of the old inhabitants have found the position very difficult. A lot more toleration is required.

The one question which crops up all the time in my correspondence on this matter is the question of Sunday observance. In every letter there is a complaint from the Christian that the Jew is doing something on a Sunday which is repugnant to the Christian inhabitants, who probably lived there long before the Jew came". HC Deb 19 May 1943 vol 389 cc1117-204

This statement clearly shows that Christians held anti-Semitic and anti-Judaic views above the primary call basic human rights which should be the basis of our faith.

Chapter 9 ~ Protestant Complicity

Catholic leaders were not the only Christians who dehumanised Jews. Protestant anti-Semites such as Adolf Stoecker also paved the way for ordinary people to carry out mass murder. Stoecker, court chaplain to Kaiser Wilhelm II, died in 1909. A Lutheran theologian and respected Christian leader, he was a staunch anti-Semite and expounded Jewish conspiracy theories. He said German culture was being Jewified ("Verjudung").

In 1879 Stoecker's speech, *"What we demand of modern Jewry,"* called for quotas for Jews and laws restricting their professional status. He demanded that Jews should not hold public office and called for Jews who held office to be stood down. He called for limitations on Jewish immigration. In his speeches and sermons, Stoecker accused Jews of leading the financial institutions for their own political ends. His incitement of hatred against Jews during the 1880s influenced the rise of anti-Semitic movements in Berlin and other German cites.

Having considered the Catholic programme of dehumanising Jews in the minds of the parents of the perpetrators, we can now observe that European Protestants, particularly in Austria and Germany, had similar programmes. Hitler was aged ten when Stoecker made his "Verjudung" speech, so we can see that many of the foundational principles for the Nuremburg Laws did not originate with him.

On 1st June 1933 Gerhard Kittel, another leading Protestant theologian, gave a lecture entitled the *"Jewish Problem."* He referred to the Jews as a racially constituted alien body within German society. He said that Jews had infected German society with their blood and spirit with calamitous consequences. He then considered four ways of dealing with the Jews and introduced the idea of "elimination of all Jewry in Europe."

In his book "Hitler's Willing Executioners," Daniel Jonah Goldhagen highlighted this speech. He wrote: *"That this eminent theologian would publicly contemplate the extermination of the Jews already in 1933 – almost in passing, without any great elaboration or justification, and as a normal, easily discussed option when trying to fashion a 'solution' to the*

'Jewish problem' – reveals the lethality of regnant eliminationist anti-Semitism, and how ordinary its discussion must have seemed to ordinary Germans in the Germany of the early 1930s."

Having studied this period of The Holocaust for many years, I can concur with the depth and meaning of Yehuda Bauer's statement in his book "A History of the Holocaust." He wrote: *"The Nazis did not add any new elements to anti-Semitism except for their determination to implement it – but the full blown anti-Semitic ideology that eventually developed combined elements of both Christian and pseudoscientific nineteenth century anti-Semitism."*

Kittel, in June 1933, placed in the minds of ordinary German Christians the idea of *"elimination"* but it wasn't until 20th January 1942 during the Wannsee Conference that Hitler put the process of the entire elimination of the Jews of Europe into action. No one can defend what happened at Wannsee, but I do believe that Kittel and Christian leaders like him watered the seeds of genocide which in part inspired what came to known as the Final Solution.

What Christendom did, in the few years prior to the war, was to reinforce the belief that Jews were less than human. Christendom convinced European society that Jews were a danger to the Church and to Germany. Europeans were led to believe that Jews were their number one enemy. This led directly to the political leaders renewing the old apostate Christian ideas of restrictive laws. Hitler introduced them at Nuremberg in 1935.

Finally, the leaders of European Christendom introduced the notion of elimination of the Jews. In short, they paved the way for genocide of the Jews. Hitler and his followers were left with the simple task of giving permission for the mass killing. Hitler turned the key on a prolonged programme by the Church to bring an end to European Jewry.

Most genocides occur when the religious leaders in a nation agree on a political murderous ideology which focuses on a minority with different views to the norm. The best example is The Holocaust whereby state and Church agreed that Jews were a danger to society and to Christendom. I view the process of mass murder of Jews in Europe during the Second World War as being one in which the Church provided the vision of genocide and the Nazis and their accomplices provided the means.

There were, of course, Protestant leaders like Lutheran theologian Dietrich Bonhoeffer. He courageously opposed the Nazi regime and was executed on 9th April 1945 for assisting in the rescue of Jews. We must remember that many clergy and ordinary Christians rescued Jews, but the vast majority of believers did not.

Historian Stephen R Haynes says: "Thousands of baptised Protestants participated as perpetrators in the Nazi Final Solution of the Jewish question. Whilst it is tempting for Christians to deny that any genuine Protestant could participate in mass murder, much less against members of God's chosen people – the fact is that persons from every Protestant tradition aided the genocide. Many Protestant Christians who did not perpetrate violence against Jews were nonetheless collaborators in Nazi anti-Semitism."

Haynes acknowledges the thousands of Protestants who helped and rescued Jews but adds: "The vast majority of Christians were neither perpetrators nor resisters but were rather bystanders who did not contribute directly to the murder of Jews but did nothing to thwart it."

Historian Victoria J Barnett writes in the book "The Holocaust and the Christian World: "In Nazi Germany in September 1935 there were a few Christians in the Protestant Confessing Church who demanded that their church take a public stand in defence of the Jews. Their efforts however were overruled by church leaders who wanted to avoid any conflict with the Nazi regime."

She also states: "Moreover and particularly in the German Evangelical Church (the largest Protestant church in Germany), the allegiance to the concept of Christendom was linked to a strong nationalism".

She continues; "Throughout the 1930s there was ample evidence of anti-Semitism in many sermons and in articles that appeared in German church publications. Some church leaders proudly announced that they were anti-Semites. Others warned their colleagues of any public show of support for the Jewish victims of the Nazi regime.

Christian anti-Semitism often complimented other factors, notably the strong Nationalism in the German Protestant churches. The most extreme example of this combination of anti-Semitism and nationalism was the so called German Christian Movement (GCM), a Protestant group that embraced Nazism and tried to 'Nazify' Christianity by suppressing the

Old Testament, revising liturgies and hymns, and promoting Jesus as an Aryan hero who embraced the ideals of the new Germany."

As we look deeper at the years of The Holocaust we can see that the Protestant churches provided records to the Nazis regarding who were Jews and who were not. Germany had a population at that time of 60 million of whom 95% had church affiliations, 60% Protestant and 35% Roman Catholic. Churches held records on their congregants and their families. The Nuremberg Laws of 1935, which Hitler copied from church councils and decrees, including that of the yellow star, relied upon religious distinctions to determine who was an Aryan or a Jew. If one's grandparents were Jewish you were considered a Jew.

The churches provided baptismal and marriage certificates, plus other documents, to prove whether a person was a Jew or Aryan. Many Jews had converted to Christianity but if the records showed they had a Jewish bloodline they were considered Jewish under the Nuremberg laws and thus destined for execution. The fact that churches provided records which condemned innocent people to certain death is no surprise. Prior to Hitler's rise to power, 70% of Protestant pastors in Germany had allied themselves to the extremely anti-Semitic National Peoples Party. Their anti-Semitism soaked into Protestant publications.

During the first months of Hitler's rule the architects for this mass murder were already gathering information for a census using an American device called a Hollerith machine. Edwin Black's book "IBM and the Holocaust" describes this machine in detail and how it was used. He wrote that on 11th June 1933 the New York Times reported that the Hollerith was being used to gather data on the 350,000 government workers in Germany to identify Jewish workers. There were other reports available at the time to show that the Nazi party was putting huge resources into identifying Jews.

Christendom obliged in the compilation of the national census. The Catholic Burial Society, the Church Council in Eisenach, the Family Baptism registry, and many Evangelical organisations provided information as to Jews who had converted to Christianity, who were half, quarter or eighth Jewish.

Black states that churches were among the leading sources for census records which went back as far as 1722. This is despite the fact that the purpose of the census was clearly known to be dangerous for Jews. A Pastor Stich complained that larger Hollerith cards were needed to contain all the data. He said: *"We are glad to serve the cause and ready to do the job right."* This search for data continued throughout all Nazi occupied countries.

Data searches were made when the Einsatzgruppen entered towns and villages. Lists of names were compiled for those to be taken to the pits for shooting or to the camps for gassing. Jews had lived in Germany since AD 400. Many had assimilated and converted to Christianity.

Imagine how it would have felt to find that, after you had been a church attendee all your life, your name was on the list. This is what happened to many Jews. Many Church leaders failed to defend them. In fact churches provided the information which condemned them.

The Protestant weekly press, with a minimum circulation of 1.8 million, gave anti-Semitic church leaders a platform to influence ordinary churchgoers. Articles asserting that Jews were the enemies of Christianity were regularly published. Bishop Otto Dibelius, of the Evangelical Lutheran Church of Prussia, declared in April 1933, shortly after the boycott of Jewish businesses, that he had always been an anti-Semite. He said: *"One cannot fail to appreciate that in all the corrosive manifestations of modern civilisation Jewry plays a leading role."*

Chapter 10 ~ Just a Few Nazi's?

During the 2015 Holocaust Remembrance Week members of my congregation surveyed nearly 300 shoppers in Liverpool city centre. Of these, 97% surveyed knew something about The Holocaust. When asked who were the perpetrators the replies were *"the Nazis"*. Those surveyed had no idea as to the extent Christendom was involved in The Holocaust nor did they have any idea that Christendom was complicit in any way.

The evidence is that church leaders like Dibelius, Archbishop Konrad Grober, Gerhard Kittel and Protestant leader Bishop Martin Sasse all incited the hatred of Jews and never spoke out against the elimination theory or its obvious manifestation. Daniel Goldhagen wrote in his book "Hitler's Willing Executioners" that the *"German churches cooperated wholeheartedly in this obviously eliminationist and lethal measure."* This statement is a chilling indictment on Christendom. It needs to be restated and understood by all of within Christendom today.

Evangelicals worldwide are now taking an interest in The Holocaust. Holocaust Remembrance Day is in the programme of many churches. The study of The Holocaust by Christians is increasing, but it is also true to say that often their main focus is on the Christian rescuers. This is a legitimate study but it does not acknowledge, or even register, the fact that every believer in Christ should know more about the Church's guilty secret. If we don't accept this fact then there may be a propensity to incite hatred against Israel. Ant-Zionism has become a feature of many Christian organisations today. Despite their protestations this is another form of anti-Semitism.

Most people today have the mistaken view that a few demon possessed mad men murdered six million Jews. Goldhagen in his book "Hitler's Willing Executioners" provides startling information based on recent research. He suggests that the German perpetrators numbered well in excess of 100,000. There were 10,005 camps which included satellite camps situated on the edges of towns and villages. Auschwitz had 50 satellite camps and more than 7,000 guards. In 1945 Dachau there were 4,100 guards and administrators. There was a ratio of one guard for every ten prisoners. This does not include administration staff and those who worked near or in the camp on general duties. These numbers provide us with a better understanding of the enormity of the Shoah and how many people knew of what was going on.

I have personal experience of UK mass police actions such as the Toxteth riots in Liverpool and the miners' strikes. Those of us involved in policing these events were not just officers standing in a line with shields at picket lines, there were support staff in the background. These included typists, secretaries, administrators, and vehicle maintenance crews. Support staff not on the front line nevertheless made it possible for front line police to function. They knew the details of our duties and the outcomes. This was the same for the German Police Battalions who murdered Jews in the killing fields by mass shootings.

Every action needed planning, backup and support staff and also the co-operation of the local community. Who typed the reports which the commanders of the death squads sent to their headquarters? Local people also buried those who were shot. Jan Grabowski in his book "Hunt for the Jews" describes that local people buried corpses in order to obtain their clothing as did the "Blue Police" who were Poland's local police force. They shot many Jews found hiding in homes and forests. Were the support staff aware of what they did?

The German Order Police Battalions were made up of ordinary policemen. They lacked army experience. Many were not Nazi party members. They were usually too old to fight and had little or no training. Yet they became the killing squads known as the Einsatzgruppen and hunted Jews who escaped.

They shot Jews at point blank range in the forests. In some cases took photographs of the executions to take home to show their families. There is one case of Police Battalion officer taking his wife on honeymoon to watch him shoot Jews. When on leave the officers told their wives and families what they had been doing.

The backup staff for these police units included administrators, those who would be responsible for the cleaning of the blood soaked uniforms, for ordering abundant drinks and food for consumption after a day's killing. There were the railway staff who accompanied the police units who guarded Jews bound for the death camps. All these knew of the killings and in one way or another played a part in the mass executions.

Many within Christendom would never imagine that clergy were involved in the police units that murdered so many civilians, but they were appointed as chaplains to the units. The chaplains looked after the spiritual needs of the units and individual men. Tadeusz Piotrowski, in his book "Poland's Holocaust" wrote: *"Surprisingly, in addition to the secular nationalist leadership, both the Ukrainian Autocephalous Orthodox Church and the Greek Catholic Church were part of this elite Nazi formation; the SS Galician."* These elite units were simply killing squads.

An article by Yithak Arad states that Archbishop Skvireckas and Bishop Vincentas Brizgys of Lithuania did not intentionally incite hatred towards Jews but they did appoint chaplains to the Lithuanian Police Battalions. The evidence is clear to me that the pair ignored the killings, which they certainly knew about, and allowed their responsibilities to fall below acceptable moral standards.

Doris L Bergen in the book "Holocaust Scholarship" wrote about reports by chaplains attached to or ministering to police units, stating: *"Military chaplains were important sources of legitimacy in yet another way. They provided a counter narrative to their brutalised surroundings. It was not atrocity in which German soldiers were involved, they preached it was duty. Germans were not killers but victims."*

Berger also wrote: "An Einsatzgruppen report from late 1941 described the killing of tens of thousands of Jews in the Baltic region and mentioned military chaplains holding services for the local Volksdeutchen" (People who were not German but spoke German, practised German culture and had German ancestry).

Grabowski quotes testimony from Abraham Mahler who claimed that the most active anti-Semites in parts of Poland, such as Dabrowa, were local priests. In the same book Grabowski relates the testimony of the death of a Pole, Josef Gribes, who rescued Jews.

At his funeral the priest refused to follow the coffin to the graveside. We must understand from all the evidence and the documentation that the murders of Jews in local communities were common knowledge.

I must mention here that the situation in Poland is extremely complex. Millions of Poles died and in his book "Poland's Holocaust" Tadeusz Piotrowski points out in a vast amount of detailed analysis that during the war 2,801 Polish Clergy were killed, either murdered or in Military manoeuvres.

There is no doubt that some of those murdered were helping Jews and Poland has the highest number of "Righteous Amongst the Nations". I must also mention however that in communications between the Churches in Poland there are no references to the plight of Jews, only Christians. Those Christians who did try to rescue Jews were focused mainly on baptised Jews and in many cases ignored the plight of non - baptised Jews.

In November 2014 I visited Neuengamme in Northern Germany, the site of a labour camp for Polish and Russian political prisoners, homosexuals and Jews. The camp was founded in 1938 and liberated by the British in 1945. It housed a total of 106,000 inmates. It had a crematorium with a tall chimney and was surrounded by a fence with turrets for security. The camp made bricks for the war effort. The inmates could be seen by passers-by, and the Lutheran Church was just three kilometres away.

I visited the archives and found a document which tied the officialdom of the Lutheran Church to the SS who ran the camp as a business. The document was the contract of sale of land in March 1944 which the church owned and had sold to the SS to enable a train line to be built making it more efficient to convey materials and prisoners. This camp was one of the many camps in Germany which at the end of the war carried out the death marches. Members of the church, as well as the Church leaders, couldn't fail to have knowledge of the atrocities which took place there.

The ordinary Christian congregants were well aware of the plight of Jews and those who had converted from Judaism. Many congregants did help, but many did not do so and made things more difficult for converts. One such case was that of Emma Becker cited in Goldhagen's book "Hitler's willing Executioners."

Emma was a Jew who married a German Roman Catholic and converted to Catholicism. In 1940 she was expelled from the choir and the church as her fellow congregants refused to sing alongside her or kneel with her at the communion table.

Goldhagen wrote: *"Becker's treatment is by no means an isolated case, for throughout Germany, Protestant and Catholic churches tried to find ways to separate converts from the larger congregation, attempts which were generally responses to ordinary Germans vocal objections to having Jews among them praying to God and taking communion."*

There were exceptions to ill treatment of converted Jews. One exception was The Dutch Church. After the initial deportation of 100,000 Jews, Catholic, mainline Protestant and Evangelical churches agreed together to oppose the further expulsion or arrest of converted Jews.

In 1940 the Dutch Reformed Church protested from the pulpits against the dismissal of Jews as civil servants. In 1941 the churches protested against the restrictions imposed on Jews. On 7th February 1942 Roman Catholics and Protestants protested against the treatment of Jews by the occupying forces. This was the first time in history that Catholics and Protestants had joined together in a protest. All denominations co-signed the protest document. In July 1942 they repeated the protest.

The result was that the Nazi occupiers accepted a concession that all those Jews who were baptised before January 1942 would be exempt from deportation. The following week the Protestant leadership asked that their letter of protest be read in the pulpits. Catholics and Calvinists agreed to do the same.

The Nazis stated that if the protest letter was not read baptised Jews would not be deported. Protestants withheld the protest to save their congregants, but the Calvinists and Catholics read out the letter. Yohannes de Jong, the Roman Catholic Archbishop of Utrecht, denounced the anti-Jewish measures as contrary to God's commands about injustice and mercy.

On 1st August 1942 the Nazis responded and 690 Catholic Jews were arrested, deported and murdered in the camps. Edith Stein, a convert from Judaism and respected theologian, was in that number. Even though promises had been made to the Dutch Reformed Church to leave their Jewish congregants alone in return for silence, 500 converted Jews were arrested and deported in September 1944.

The Hungarian Church also tried to prevent the deportations of converted Jews but it is clear that their leaders lacked the courage to speak out openly against their own government and the Nazi occupiers.

Chapter 11 ~ German Christians

The most active anti-Semitic Christian organisation in Germany and Austria was the German Christian Movement (GCM). This movement of Protestant Christians began with ideas in 1920s of integrating the Protestant Church with German culture and ethnicity. Pastors Siegfried Leffler and Julius Leutheuser preached about religious renewal along nationalistic lines. Both were Nazi party members who said German Protestants should support its ideology.

In 1932 these pastors met clergy and politicians in Berlin to discuss how the Protestant Church could be invigorated into action in conjunction with the National Socialist cause. By the mid-thirties this movement had more than 500,000 members who fully endorsed the Nazi ideology. Ludwig Muller, a military chaplain in the First World War, was appointed German Christian Protestant Reich Bishop in 1933.

Muller was an associate of Hitler and a member of the Nazi party and, of course, an anti-Semite. Muller said in 1934: "We must emphasise with all decisiveness that Christianity did not grow out of Judaism but developed in opposition to Judaism." In 1939 Muller called for a ban on Jewish influence in all areas of German life, including the Church.

n 13th November 1933 another leader in the movement, Reinhold Krause, another Nazi party member, addressed a rally of 20,000 members at the Sports Palace in Berlin. Krause spoke against many of the fundamental ideas in Christianity, stating that they were influenced by Jewish practice. He regarded the Old Testament as an unacceptable remnant of Judaism. The speech became a divisive issue but the reality in Germany was that the Old Testament faded from readings and sermons.

A must read for anyone interested in German Christians in the Nazi era is a book written by Doris L Bergen called the "Twisted Cross." Bergen highlighted the 10 guidelines/principles published by the GCM in 1932. These anti-Jewish principles involved ideas of race. Principle seven stated that the mixing of race was to be opposed. Principle nine called for marriage between Jews and Germans to be forbidden. This was before the Nazi Nuremburg Laws and before Hitler's appointment as Chancellor early in 1933. Referring to the 10 principles, Bergen observes. *"Even before Nazis took power, the German Christians had concretized their views of race and its place within the Church."*

The question of whether Jews who had converted to Christianity were still Jews was a hotly debated subject throughout all denominations. In 1933 German Christian Freidrich Wieneke demanded a truly German Church based on blood and not baptism. This view opened the door to removing Jews from churches. In 1937 there were more calls for a Jew-free Church.

In April 1939, 11 regional GCM churches signed the "Godesburg Declaration" stating that Christianity was the religious opposite of Judaism and announced the creation of the Institution for Research into and Elimination of Jewish Influence in German Church life.

During two teaching periods in Bremen, Germany, I learned that Jews from the city and Hamburg were transported to Minsk, Belarus, during the war where they were murdered by shooting. I was told that many Bremen Christians gave food and clothing to these Jews not knowing they were going to be killed.

My research revealed that Bremen and Hamburg men who were too old for the German army, and who were not members of the Nazi party, joined police units during the war and operated in Ukraine and other German occupied countries. These units were made up of ordinary men from ordinary backgrounds who voluntarily shot Jews – men, women and children – at point blank range in the forests, towns and cities to which they were sent. How could it be that these ordinary men became, as Daniel Jonah Goldhagen entitled his book "Hitler's Willing Executioners?" I asked myself. Many were Protestants who attended church regularly.

My question may be answered in some way by looking at the religious influence on those who served in the police battalions known as 'Order Police'. Early in 1942 the Protestant Bishop of Bremen, Heinz Weidmann, declared his church, and those within his diocese, *"officially anti-Jewish."* He was an active member of the German Christian Movement and a member of the Nazi party. He was fervently opposed to all Jewish influences in the Protestant Church. He removed teaching from the Old Testament and spent a great deal of time during the 1930s removing as many references as he could from the various versions of the gospels and hymns. Doris Bergen's "Twisted Cross" book states of him: *"His aggressive anti-Jewish stance found support far beyond Bremen."*

This was also a period when German clergy advocated the removal of non-Aryans from their ranks and their parishioners rejected the Old Testament. Meanwhile, the Nuremburg Laws removed German citizenship from Jews. The Confessing Church was also silent regarding the GCM view of race. Many Lutherans associated with the Confessing Church did not oppose the GCM's anti-Semitism. Although Lutheran Pastor Martin Niemoller, who spent seven years in concentration camps because of his opposition to Hitler, opposed the plans to eject non Aryans from the Church, he still professed he was an anti-Semite. When the non-Aryan controversy within the Church was discussed, Niemoller suggested those with Jewish ancestry holding church office should resign to spare their Christian brothers having to make difficult decisions.

In 1934 a church in Saxony denied the use of a building to a Christian choir because its choirmaster had converted as a Jew to Christianity.

In 1936 German Christians celebrated the third anniversary of the Nazi revolution. They sang a hymn proclaiming Nazi beliefs to be a divine revelation and Hitler to be God's emissary on Earth. This is despite the fact that Hitler had implemented sterilisation and racist laws. This theme was developed in GCM's new hymns and liturgies.

In 1942, Pastor Julius Leutheuser declared that the word Fuhrer meant *"he who has led us to God."* GCM referred to their meetings not as worship services but divine celebrations. In the same year Wilhelm Staedel, a Lutheran GCM pastor in Romania, established "The German Christian Institute into the Elimination of Jewish Influence" in the country.

In 1938 Bishop Helmut Johnsen excluded two pastors from churches under his jurisdiction because their mothers were Jewish. In 1939 Protestant Church authorities in Prussia called for all ordination candidates to prove they did not have Jewish blood. They investigated the ancestry of all their pastors and their wives to ensure they were not in any way Jewish.

One of GCM's main goals was to remove any idea that Christianity was in any way connected to Judaism. Hermann Werdermann, a professor at the teachers' college in Dortmund and a member of the movement, opposed Judaism and the Old Testament. GCM leaders reviewed more than 2,000 hymns in an attempt to remove those which contained anything which could be considered Jewish. They eliminated all but 105 from their lists. In 1939 Bishop Weidmann of Bremen released a new German hymn book. Immediately it sold thousands of copies. The hymn book was popularised by it being Judaism free. A hymn book for Protestant soldiers free of all references to Jews and Jerusalem was distributed to the military. This had been a long-term goal of GCM leader Krause who said in 1933: *"We want to sing songs that are free from all Israelite elements."*

After the Old Testament had been removed, Bishop Weidman of Bremen published the first anti-Jewish scripture –"The German Gospel of John" in 1936. Doris Bergen in her book "The Twisted Cross" describes the publication as an onslaught against Judaism.

In 1939 the German Christian Institute for Research into Elimination of Jewish Influence in German Church Life" produced the first anti-Semitic gospels called "The Message of God." This version removed such verses as *"Forgive them for they know not what they do"* (Luke 23: 34). Over 200,000 copies of "The Message of God" were sold within six months. Clergy were encouraged to teach from it in their sermons.

Bergen also refers to a Catholic priest who was a prominent GCM activist who released a brochure called "The Sermon on the Mount as a declaration of war against Judaism."

A new catechism removed many tenets of the Christian faith and a new set of commandments were made which are as follows:

1. Honour God and believe in him wholeheartedly.

2. Seek out the peace of God.

3. Avoid all hypocrisy.

4. Holy is your health and life.

5. Holy is your well-being and honour.

6. Holy is your truth and fidelity.

7. Honour your father and mother—your children are your aid and your example.

8. Keep the blood pure and the marriage holy.

9. Maintain and multiply the heritage of your forefathers.

10. Be ready to help and forgive.

11. Honour your Führer and master.

12. Joyously serve the people with work and sacrifice.

Today we can see that these documents are a deception and can easily be proven as fabrications. However we have to remember that the Christian pulpit and pew during this period had been raised on a series of lies about Jews and Judaism. Their parents had handed down to them stories demonising Jews and Judaism. They had been brainwashed into believing that Jews were an enemy of God and enemy of the Church. When GCM publications, which removed anything Jewish, went on sale ordinary people accepted them as being the true writings of the Apostles.

Many articles were written by leading theologians or bishops. Place yourself in the position of being a Protestant Lutheran farmer, policeman, civil servant or teacher in Bremen during the 1930s and early 1940s. Your bishop publishes new texts which he states are the true word of God. I guess many accepted them because people usually accept what those in authority state .Many churchgoers then and now do not know the Bible as well as they should to enable them to judge whether what is being taught lines up with Scripture.

Many churches today do not properly teach the Scriptures. Many churches falsely preach that God did not promise the Land of Israel to Jews alone. They support Arab claims for the Holy Land despite the Bible stating it rightfully belongs to Jews. The same scenario affected the ordinary pre-war church attendees. They accepted anti-Semitism as the norm. GCM leaders set the agenda and their many adherents followed through their plan by becoming the killers of European Jews.

Chapter 12 ~ Massacres in German-Occupied Countries

During a teaching assignment in Minsk, Belarus, I was given a guided tour by Holocaust survivor Frida Reyzman. With my colleague and friend Keith Darnell I was taken to memorials in two former Jewish ghettos in the city. More than 19,000 Jews were murdered in these ghettos. We heard that a church was just 700 metres away and that the Christian population witnessed all that went on. We later visited the two former Jewish ghettos in Vilnius, Lithuania, which were overlooked by churches on the boundaries. Jews had died within hearing distance of Christian worshippers.

In many other Eastern European countries local men rounded up Jews and murdered them. Ordinary men, as well as local police officers, in Ukraine, Latvia, Lithuania and Prussia killed with enthusiasm believing this was the will of the Church and God. Many were churchgoers who saw their role as assistant executioners a legitimate Christian act. They had been taught in church that Jews were enemies of Roman Catholicism. In 1936, Cardinal Hlond of Poland said Jews *"were the vanguard of atheism."* He encouraged the boycott of Jewish business and warned that the Jews were *"waging war against the Catholic Church."*

This teaching of hatred encouraged communities to work voluntarily with the German Police Battalions. Daniel Jonah Goldhagen's book "Hitler's Willing Executioners" and Christopher R Browning's book "Ordinary Men" detail the origins and work of the battalions that committed murders in occupied territories or oversaw the mass murders. Stephen C Smith's publication "The Holocaust Guide for Police Personnel" highlights Reserve Battalion 101. Browning's book describes in graphic detail this battalion's role in the mass murders and deportation murders.

These battalions were made up of ordinary men who were farmers and part-time police officers and not members of the Nazi party. They had no desire to fight in the army and were not politically minded. Many of these men were church attendees from across the denominations. The Protestant, Catholic, and Evangelical Church members had been exposed from childhood to anti-Semitism. Seventy per cent of their clergy had anti-Semitic attitudes and were determined to pass on their views to their congregations. Many of those who joined the battalions were already equipped with the armoury of hatred towards Jews and were vulnerable to the Nazi policy of elimination of Jews. These battalions, known as Order Police, were formed into units of the infamous Einsatzgruppen (task forces) under the command of the Waffen SS.

Battalion 101 had less than 500 men, mainly from Hamburg, many of whom were aged in their forties with no military experience. They were sent into Poland in 1939 where they guarded Polish prisoners of war. They returned to Hamburg to be re-formed and trained at various times during the war. They were involved in rounding up Jews from the Hamburg and Bremen areas. The Jews were put on east-bound trains destined to be shot at camps in Lodz, Minsk and Riga. In 1942 the battalion guarded Lodz Ghetto. During the war Battalion 101 members shot, at point blank range, Jewish men, women and children. The killings culminated in the "Harvest Festival Massacre" on 3rd and 4th November 1943 in the Lublin district of Poland. Some 42,000 Jewish men women and children were forced to strip and walk naked before they were shot by the battalion. This battalion of police reservists, many of whom attended church, were responsible for the murders of 83,000 Jews. Major Wilhelm Trapp, the battalion commander, was executed for war crimes in December 1948. Only five battalion members were convicted of crimes at court trials in 1967, the longest prison sentence being eight years. The majority of these police officers returned to their families and churches without further mention of the terrible crimes they committed. Silence was their friend. Wives, children, and clergy dared not speak about the crimes they knew must have taken place.

How did these ordinary men commit such terrible crimes? As a police detective I was involved in a number of murder cases varying from domestic murders to violent attacks. In many of these cases the killers had, in their own minds, dehumanised the victim. This process often takes place to enable one human being to kill another. German churches had over many years dehumanised the Jew. Political forces under the command of Hitler stepped up that dehumanising process. This resulted in Christian men shooting Jews, fellow human beings, at close range. In other words, Christendom was a willing conspirator with the Nazi regime, counselling and procuring vast numbers of otherwise ordinary people to commit mass murder. Battalion 101 was simply a product of the dehumanising process.

In Poland, local people were used to exterminate the country's three million Jews. The nation's Blue Police worked closely with the German Order Police to round up Jews. The Blue Police were excellent at gathering information as to the hiding places of Jews as they were from the same localities. They knew the area's geography and had good local contacts. The Germans used this to their advantage and got the Blue Police to hunt for Jews who, when found, were taken to police stations and shot by the Order Police.

Local people then buried the dead. If local communities were so involved how could the churches not know what was going on? I was a police officer in a large village. The vicar was a friend and would tell me he knew nearly everything I was doing because of what his parishioners told him. I knew what the vicar was doing too because of the villagers' information. We both knew the local undertaker well and picked up information from him, as we did with the postman and doctor.

I find it impossible to believe that during the mass executions in Poland priests did not know that parishioners were murdering their Jewish neighbours. Bishops and other senior clergy also knew the tragic facts but said nothing. There were no instructions from the Vatican to local priests as to how to respond to the killings. In part, because local priests had no guidelines from their hierarchy, it is true to say that with few exceptions they did nothing at all to help Jews. In some cases they assisted in the roundup of Jews and benefitted materially from their deaths as did many others.

There were also instances where individuals reported the mass murders directly to churches. Kurt Gerstein joined the Waffen SS in 1942 as an officer. A member of the Institute for Hygiene, he signed up to find out if the rumours were true about the murder of patients with physical and mental problems. In summer 1942 he visited the Nazi death camps of Belzec and Treblinka and witnessed the murder of thousands of Jews. He managed to get detailed information to the Swedish government but ministers kept it secret because they didn't want to anger Nazi Germany.

Gerstein then persuaded the Dutch Resistance to broadcast the information to the British Government by radio. Even though the British Foreign Office was aware of the murders they dismissed the reports as exaggerated and untrue, and the British government refused to react on the information. As a result the murder of millions of Jews continued unchallenged. Finally, Gerstein reported all the facts to the Roman Catholic and Protestant authorities in Berlin but they also failed to speak out against the killings. A despairing Gerstein committed suicide in 1945 because no-one acted on the information he had provided.

W. A. Hooft, a Protestant theologian and first secretary of the World Council of Churches, lived in Switzerland during the War. In October 1941 a Swiss businessman told him that he had been invited by German officers to watch the shootings of Jews. He gave a full report to Hooft who failed to act on the information.

After the war, Hooft faced up to realities of the evidence he had harboured, and wrote in his memoirs: "That moment occurred when I heard a young Swiss businessman tell what he had seen with his own eyes during a business trip to Russia. He had been invited by German officers to be present at one of the mass killings of Jews. He told us in the most straightforward and realistic way how group after group of Jewish men, women and children were forced to lie down in the mass graves and were then machine-gunned to death. The picture he drew has remained in my mind ever since. From that moment onward I had no longer any excuse for shutting my mind to information which could find no place in my view of the world and humanity."

I find it disturbing that Hooft did nothing at the time to disseminate the information he was given. He should have demanded that the governments of the world do something on behalf the Jews, but did nothing at all to prevent further murders. It was only after the war that he acknowledged that he was privy to what was happening to the Jews.

LITHUANIA

The Holocaust in Lithuania is a subject which cannot be forgotten. There were 220,000 Jews living in Lithuania when German forces invaded in June 1941. From July 1941 to 1944, some 70,000 Jews were murdered in a forested area known as Ponary just outside Vilnius.

Only 10,000 Lithuanian Jews were alive when the war ended, a great number of those surviving in the death camps in Poland and Estonia. There is evidence that before the arrival of the German forces into Lithuania mass shootings of Jews were taking place by local police units.

The evidence we have today makes it very clear that Lithuanian churches were not only complicit in the murder of Jews but actually involved in the process of "the teaching of hatred" which led to the persecution of both Jews and the Polish community, including Polish clergy.

Joseph Foxman, a survivor of the Vilnius Ghetto, wrote a book entitled "In the Shadow of Death." His son, Abraham, who recently retired after 50 years as director of the Anti-Defamation League, made some interesting points in the book's foreword. Joseph and his wife Helen asked a Roman Catholic lady to look after Abraham, only a few months old then, in the hope of them surviving the murders and harsh conditions in the ghetto. The lady baptised Abraham and re-named him Henryk Stanislaw Kurpi and brought him up in the Roman Catholic Church. Abraham wrote: *"I would cross myself when I passed a church. When I met a priest I kissed his hand; when I saw a Jew I had been taught to spit at him."* This is indicative of the teaching of hatred being the norm within the Catholic community at the time.

On a visit to Vilnius, Lithuania, with Keith Darnell, we were struck by the fact that the two former ghettos in the city had churches situated alongside them. The ghetto that ran along Rudnicki Street had the Church of All Saints across the street. The church was illuminated at night and had a large sign which read *"Bringing foodstuffs into the ghetto is strictly forbidden. Anyone found guilty of violating this regulation will receive the death penalty. By Order of the Commandant of the City."* Residents of the city, including clergy and their congregations, would have witnessed the starvation and acts of inhumanity taking place in the ghetto. We cannot speculate as to why individual Christians did not actually help the Jews because we don't know what pressure they may have been under from the German occupiers. However, we can say that their bishops could have acted differently and not incited the hatred of Jews or supported the Nazis, and certainly should not have remained silent.

Dr. Arūnas Streikus conducted a research project entitled "The Catholic Church as Institution during the Period of the Nazi Occupation of Lithuania." In his conclusions he explained that Archbishop Skvireckas wrote in his diary for 30 June 1941:

"The thoughts of Mein Kampf concerning the poisonous Bolshevik influence exercised by Jews on the nations of the world are worthy of note. These thoughts are interesting indeed. They are true to life and present an insight into reality. Whether it belongs to Hitler himself or to

his associates is hard to say. But all this testifies to Hitler being not only an enemy of the Jews, but to the correctness of his thoughts as well."

Why would an intelligent Christian leader with great authority recommend such a racist book as Hitler's Mein Kampf? The book expresses hatred against the Jewish people and accuses them of conspiracies against the rest of the world. Skvireckas was clearly anti-Semitic, and with such statements promulgating hatred against the Jews on a huge scale he is clearly complicit in the murders.

Yitak Arad's paper "Defending History" features the Lithuanian Church leadership and points out that the Roman Catholic Church provided no assistance to the Jewish community, not even allowing them to convert. He wrote: *"On 8 April 1942 the leadership of the church in Kaunas sent a memorandum to priests which sought to prevent altogether or to make it more difficult for Jews to get baptised as any kind of an aid to survival. The memo added: "With a view of avoiding possible disturbances and even sacrilege of sacred matters, the Ordinariate, re-establishing the order that existed until present in the Archdiocese, resolves that holy baptism shall not be administered to the individuals of the Jewish origin without an appropriate thorough investigation."*

Arad's book "The Holocaust in the Soviet Union" is a must read for anyone interested in the German occupation of Communist Eastern Europe. In a paper for Yad Vashem he states: *"The Catholic Church in Lithuania was also in an influential position, which could have been used to help the Jews in view of the large-scale participation of Lithuanian police battalions in the anti-Jewish actions, even outside Lithuania. A further indication of the Church's involvement was that Lithuanian chaplains served in some of these 'units of death.' The Lutheran Church in Latvia and Estonia assumed a similar attitude. In these Baltic countries the ruling churches remained silent."*

"The Eastern European Churches and the Holocaust," written by Gerald Darring, again points to the complicity of church leaders in Lithuania. He wrote: *"Lithuanians, 95 per cent of whom were Catholics, welcomed the Germans as liberators and more often than not were willing collaborators in gathering and killing Jews. In fact, Lithuanian Catholics tortured and killed Jews in at least 40 communities even before the German army arrived."*

Bishop Vincentas Brizgys was the chief spokesman for the RC Church in

Lithuania. He sent a telegram congratulating the Nazis on their success in Lithuania. A delegation of Jewish leaders met with Brizgys, pleading with him to intervene in the rounding up and shooting of Jews. He refused, saying that he could not accept responsibility for endangering the church by helping the Jews.

The chief of the Security Police and the SD (Intelligence Services) included the following in his "Operational Situation Report USSR No. 54," dated August 16, 1941: *"Organisation of the Catholic Church in Lithuania. The attitude of the church regarding the Jewish question is, in general, clear. In addition, Bishop Brisgys has forbidden all clergymen to help Jews in any form whatsoever. He rejected several Jewish delegations which approached him personally and asked for his intervention with the German authorities. In the future he will not meet with any Jews at all. Conversion of Jews to the Catholic faith did not take place so far. The church would also object to this type of conversion"*

Many bystanders also benefited from the murder of men women and children by becoming the new owners of victims' homes. They also gained from selling clothing and personal belongings, many of which were taken from the bodies of those who had been shot. Many sold the property of the victims, and many extracted large amounts of money and personal belongings from Jews, particularly in return for hiding them.

Once the money ran out they reported their whereabouts to the Einsatzgruppen or local police who arrested and shot them. This was the case in Poland, Lithuania and other German occupied areas. There are, of course, many reasons why we shouldn't harshly judge bystanders during these times, but the fact remains that many did nothing to stop or report the killings because they were receiving benefits from the mass murders.

Brisgys is also mentioned in a bystander's diary written by Kazimierz Sakowizc, a journalist who lived at Ponary, Lithuania. He wrote about his witness of the thousands of Jews who were stripped of their clothing and shot on the edges of pits. Sakowizc's account of what he saw between 1941 and 1943 is written in a matter of fact style without emotion about those he referred to as *"the condemned."* It is a valuable unbiased account of the actual events. Sakowizc did not survive the war but parts of his diary which he hid in various places, mainly in glass bottles, did. This is what he said about Bishop Vincentas Brisgys of Kovno in February 1943 when it was clear that the Russian army was advancing to take back control of Lithuania: *"The day before yesterday Radio London announced, citing Stockholm, that the Bishop of Kovno said that it is not the obligation of Lithuanians to kill Jews and Poles, and in any case he condemned and forbade it." I do not believe that this happened. Why did the bishop fail to condemn Germans and Lithuanians when they were killing priests, when they took away the Archbishop, when they were torturing and murdering Poles? But now, when there are defeats in Libya and Tripoli; when Stalingrad, Rostov, Kursk, Kharkov have fallen; when the Germans are encircled in the Caucasus and threatened in the Crimea, only then does the bishop 'condemn' because he sees a foretaste of the defeat of the Lithuanians, who more than any other nation in the world, have so many murders in their conscience. Before this he did not prohibit the murders, because then they suited his purpose, to cleanse the church of Poles."* I have just obtained a document which shows that Brisgys spent his post years in comfort in America having evaded prosecution or disclosure of his failure to act to stop the obvious atrocities taking place under his nose.

It is abundantly clear that Brisgys was looking after his own position and that the Lithuanian community saw through it. Many Polish RC clergy in Lithuania were also murdered, not only by the German Order Police but by Lithuanian police officers. Sakowizc's diary contains first-hand information about the murder of Polish clergy in the pits of Ponary and how they, like the thousands of Jews, were forced to remove their clothing before being shot. Many Lithuanian clergy helped in the murders. Many clergy were attached to the police battalions and even blessed them before they went out to murder.

UKRAINE

Ukraine also saw similar examples of direct clergy complicity in the murders. Again clergy were attached to the local killing squads and blessed the men. Yitzhak Arad highlights an incident in which clergy attached to the killing squads attempted to protect the so called honour of the German police battalions. Arad wrote: *"The first city in Generalbezirk Kiev where an extermination action took place was Belaya Tserkov. The pre-war Jewish population there had been 9,500 and after its fall on July 16, 1941, an estimated 5,000 to 6,000 remained. The town's entire Jewish population was annihilated in mid-August. According to a report from Feldkommandantur in Belaya Tserkov to Security division 454, dated September 11, 1941, "Many of the Jews in Belaya Tserkov were shot. All the others escaped. In fact, no more Jews remain there."*

After the extermination of the town's Jews, 100 Jewish children were found in one of the vacated apartments. Two German documents record the fate of these children. An August 21, 1941, report from the Chaplain of 295 Infantry Division to Lt. Col. Helmuth at Division HQ stated:

"Yesterday, August 20, at about 15:00, the division's Catholic priest and I were visited by two priests from the nearby field hospital. They told us that about 500 metres from here, they found between 80 and 90 babies and children under school age in one of the buildings. Their shouts and weeping could be heard a long way off ... I went with the two priests and my friend the Catholic priest to this house and saw children sitting and lying down in two small rooms – some in their own filth – and the main thing is that there was not a drop of drinking water and the children were terribly thirsty. A Ukrainian policeman was guarding them. We learned from him that these are Jewish children whose parents had been shot. A group of German soldiers stood around the house, and the two discussed excitedly what they had seen and heard. Since I assume that it is undesirable for such things to become common knowledge, I am reporting it.

"That day, the division's commander sent a report to the commander of the Sixth Army, Generalfeldmarschall von Reichenau, who ordered EK 5 commander Blobel to leave immediately for Belaya Tserkov with the Sixth Army representative to assess the situation. At the same time, he decided that 'the action that had begun had to be completed, but in a suitable manner.' The meaning of this decision was that the murder of the last remaining children must be continued. Obersturmfuhrer August Hafner of Sonderkommando 4a, who participated in the execution of the children, testified: 'Blobel ordered me to execute the children.' I asked him: 'Who is going to carry out the shooting?' He replied: 'The Waffen-SS.' I said to him: 'They are all young people. How can we explain to them that they are to shoot small children?' ... I suggested that the execution be carried out by the Ukrainian police, under the command of the Feldkommandantur. No one opposed this suggestion ... I set off for the woods ... Soldiers had already dug the pit and they were shot ... I remember especially a little blonde girl who grabbed my hand. She, too, was shot. Some of the children had to be shot four or five times."

These priests had the option to complain about the brutality and inhumanity in this situation. They chose not to side with accepted moral standards but to try to protect the so called honour of the German killing squads. This report provides us with the depth of evil which was in the Church during these times and the effectiveness of Christian anti-Semitism which, over a prolonged period of time, turned even clergymen into persecutors.

Mordechai Paldiel wrote in his book "Churches and the Holocaust: "In 1942 Clerics of the Autocephalous Orthodox Church openly called on their flocks not to assist Jews. Such as the call to a priest in Koval in May, 1942, not to provide Jews with bread, water and shelter and to inform the Germans about any Jews hiding, for he stated Jews were to be wiped off the face of the earth. On the eve of the liquidation of the city's Jews a special thanksgiving prayer was held in church by Ivan Gruba, in which God and Hitler were spoken of in one breath. After being sprinkled with holy water, Ukrainian policemen left the church to launch a killing spree on the city's Jews. There were only a few clerics in the Ukraine who helped Jews, a few lone voices in a sea of hatred spawned from the pulpits of many churches."

Our words can have an effect on others, particularly when we are in authority in some way or other. I have been a pastor for nearly 15 years and know that what I say has some bearing on the lives of others. Whenever I preach I make it very clear that everyone must check what I say lines up with Scripture. That also applies to what you read in this book.

CROATIA

During the war in Bosnia in 1993 I took aid to a Croatian refugee camp called Gaza near to Karlovac. I supported both Croatian Catholic and Muslim refugees. In 2005 whilst studying at Yad Vashem I met an Orthodox Serbian priest who told me about a Croatian extermination camp called Jasenovac. I didn't realise until then that in 1993 I was only few miles from the most grotesque centre of murder in all of The Holocaust. I had no idea then that Croatia had any connection with The Holocaust.

I learned that the Catholic community in Croatia were involved in the murder of not only thousands of Jews but thousands of Serbs as well. Anti-Semitism in the Croatian Catholic Church led to the murder of the Jews of Croatia. In 1942 the Bishop of Sarajevo, Ivan Saric, even justified the persecution of Jews, stating that they were the descendants of those Jews that had murdered Jesus. He declared: *"Their appetite grows so that only domination of the world will satisfy it ... Satan helped them to invent Socialism and Communism."*

Besides the Jasenovac murder camp, there were five smaller camps in various other places in Croatia. The town of Jasenovac is situated just a few miles from the capital city of Zagreb on the banks of the Sava River. During the early part of 1941 the Ustashe -- the Croatian army -- complied with the racial laws against Jews, Serbs and Gypsies. The Ustashe began murdering these minorities in the camps.

There is a long standing dispute regarding the numbers murdered at Jasenovac and its satellite camps. Serb sources suggest there was a total of 700,000 murdered at Jasenovac. Croatian and other historical sources speak in terms of 85,000. It is largely accepted, though, that about 20,000 of the 32,000 Croatian Jews were murdered there. The remaining Jews were sent by transport to other death camps to be gassed.

The Jews at Jasenovac were murdered in a most brutal way. Ustashe soldiers used specially designed knives which were attached to the wrist to prevent straining. This enabled long periods of murder to take place. The head of the chaplaincy for the camp was Franciscan Friar Tomislav Filipović, who, in the name of Jesus, ordered the murder of men, women and children. He blessed the Ustashe and gave them communion before the terrible murder actions, some of which took place in and around churches. A chilling report of one of Filipović's actions is described in the book "Magnum Crimen" by Viktor Novak.

He writes: *"A brother of the Petrićevac Monastery, Tomislav Filipović, entered the classroom during class with 12 Ustashe, imitating Jesus Christ and his 12 Apostles. He ordered teacher Dobrila Martinović to bring a Serb child to the front of the class. The brother gently received the child, lifted her to the lectern and then slowly began to slit her throat in front of the other children, the teacher and the Ustashe. The brother calmly and in Jesuit-like dignified fashion addressed the Ustashe; 'Ustashe, by this in the name of God, I baptise these degenerates and you should follow my example. I am the first to accept all sin onto my soul; I will confess you and absolve you of all sin.' In the schoolyard, on the trodden snow, he placed the 12 Ustashe in a circle and then ordered the children to run next to them. As each child passed, an Ustashe would gouge out an eye and push it into the child's slit belly; he would cut off an ear from a second, the nose from a third, a finger from a fourth, and the cheeks from a fifth. ... And so on until all the children collapsed. Then the Ustashe finished them off in the snow."*

Filipović was expelled from the Catholic order two months later but was never defrocked. He became the leader of the camp, blessing and giving communion to those soldiers who carried out the murders, many of which happened in churches. A total of 2,730 Serbs, including 500 children, died at their hands on the very day Victor Novak described.

The seeds of this brutality were formed 2,000 years ago when the Early Church made Jews an enemy when they should have been friends and family. Judaism's laws were seen as disease to be feared. The Nazi regime embraced the long-held lie that Jews were a danger to society and particularly so to Germany. Church leaders and the Nazis dehumanised the Jew. As Jonathan Sacks wrote in his recent book "Not in God's Name: *"Dehumanisation destroys empathy and sympathy. It shuts down the emotions that prevent us from doing harm."*

For nearly 2,000 years Christian anti-Semitism has varied in temperature from simmering to boiling. This cauldron only boils over into mass murder when other ingredients in the form of politics or an ideology are added. The Nazi ideology was added to the cauldron of hatred and the result was an uncontrollable volcanic eruption of hatred so cruel that ordinary men and women descended into depravity that beforehand was unimaginable.

Yes, of course, there were Christians who gave their lives to save not only Jews but many other Nazi victims. However, the vast majority did nothing to help the Jews. The same applies to many national governments who simply looked on despite a plethora of intelligence detailing the Nazi genocide.

Chapter 13 ~ The 8-Step Process

There are eight steps to every genocide. Each of these stages was applicable to the genocide of European Jewry during the Second World War. The eight stages are:

1. Classification. Categories are formulated enabling an "us and them" perception. The categories are race, religion or nationality. Christendom, having broken away from its Hebraic roots, turned Jews into 'them' and defined Judaism as an unrelated religion. Christendom under the dominance of the Roman emperors classified biblical Judaism as an anathema and Jews as people of the Devil. Christendom taught that the Church had replaced the Jews and the Old Testament laws of God. This teaching continued during the war and is still prevalent today.

2. Symbolism. Once a classification is made of a people group an assigned symbols is designated to them. Diaspora Jews were given a dress code or identity mark. The Church Council of Oxford in 1222 assigned the mark of a yellow star to Jews. This sign was used to identify the Jews of Europe in 1939.

3. Dehumanisation. This process is necessary for a change in attitude for those who are being conditioned to commit atrocities. Ordinary men and women are not generally disposed to murder. However, once they are brainwashed into believing that this other person is a danger to them or their community, nation or religion then that enemy becomes sub-human and the desire to eliminate them develops. The teaching of hate or the teaching of fear of another people group creates a desire to kill. The Early Church fathers called Jews Devil's advocates, rats and vermin.

Luther compounded these ideas in the 16th century, ordering the destruction of Jewish literature, Scripture commentaries and synagogues. At the end of the 19th century Protestant and Roman Catholic Church leaders spoke of Jews as enemies. Some Christian leaders, such as the Protestant theologian Gerhard Kittel in 1933, were espousing ideas of elimination of European Jews because they were a problem to society. Pulpit teaching of Jews as enemies was the norm in most of the German occupied territories.

4. Organisation. Organisations moving towards genocide can be official or unofficial. They can be political, racial or religious. They organise and plan genocide and look towards logistics to foresee possibilities. Christendom is an official group of different organisations with a chain of command down to local clergy who then exercise power over the membership. In Germany, 95 per cent of the population had church affiliation. Clergy, not only in Germany but other occupied countries, assisted the Nazis. They rounded up Jews in their communities enabling the murderer to kill in an orderly fashion. Some clergy became chaplains of the police battalions who shot Jews and others deemed enemies. Chaplains blessed the killing squads before they carried out their crimes.

5. Polarisation. Organisations moving towards genocide drive the intended victims further away from the mainstream group. They advocate laws to isolate the intended target. Throughout history Christendom's canon laws prevented Jews from assimilating or living freely in nations. Christian leaders in Europe called for special laws to restrict the rights of Jews before Hitler's enactment of the racial laws. In fact, Hitler used Christendom's apostate teaching to introduce statutes known as the Nuremburg Laws. He only repeated the enactments against Jews created by Christendom throughout its history, a ban on Jews marrying Gentiles, wearing of the yellow star, restrictions in the workplace, and professional isolation being just a few.

6. Preparation. The preparation of genocide involves the physical separation of the target group from the community. In The Holocaust, ghettos had been created and Jews were forced to live in them totally isolated from other citizens. This physical movement of Jews from their homes into ghettos was encouraged by many leaders in Christendom who called Jews dirty and a danger to society. Many ghettos were situated near to churches. There was little or no opposition in Christendom to prevent this. In fact some senior clergy called on their congregations not to help Jews to escape the ghetto.

7. Extermination. Genocide is the extermination of a people group. Christendom has slaughtered millions of Jews throughout its 2,000 years. In the first few centuries Christians burned synagogues, and in the name of Jesus destroyed Jewish communities. The Crusades followed and then the inquisitions in Spain, Portugal, and on the Indian sub-continent.

We might be offended by the fact that Christians played an active part in the murder of innocent Jews right down to recent times, but they did. Many of Holocaust murders were carried out in the name of Jesus, the most prominent examples being in the murder camps of Croatia. The leader of the cruellest camp in all of Europe at that time was a Roman Catholic friar. Clergy were accomplices in roundups of Jews and helped to calm Jews prior to the shootings in Ukraine and Lithuania.

8. Denial. Denying involvement in genocide is a sure sign of complicity. This is where I began in this book. In Christendom we are never told of the involvement of Christians in The Holocaust or the fuelling of this terrible stain in our history. The Vatican refuses to release details of its records of the period, and ministers of religion are silent about what they witnessed, and some clergy even helped Holocaust perpetrators to escape justice after the war. My teaching of such involvement by Christians in the murder of Jews is becoming more acceptable in some areas of Europe but is still generally shut out of most churches. Evidence of complicity is only now beginning to permeate in some Christian organisations but is challenged at every stage.

As you have considered evidence of Christian complicity in The Holocaust you will have understood that Christendom had a formative role in each one of these eight stages which resulted in the murder of two-thirds of European Jewry. This makes Christendom an accomplice in the genocide we now know as The Holocaust.

SILENCE

After the war those who committed these terrible crimes naturally kept silent about their acts. They feared prosecution and being found out by their families. They also wanted to keep secret their crimes out of shame and guilt. There were those who had benefited from the mass murders of Jews because they stole property, homes, artefacts and treasures and didn't want to return them. Sadly, some of these were priests or in high position posts within society. I recently met a Lutheran minister from a town near Hamburg whose church was less than two miles from a large wartime labour camp in which there was a crematorium. Local Lutherans saw many camp inmates die and also witnessed the death marches from the camp at the end of the war. The wartime congregation and the minister of the church could not have been ignorant of the atrocities in the camp. I asked if there was any reflection by the congregation in the years immediately after the war regarding the atrocities. The minister explained that his predecessor had succeeded the minister who was the incumbent during the war. His predecessor had explained that when he took over, neither the departing minister, nor members of the congregation during the Nazi years, would talk about the camp or what they witnessed. I am sure they remained silent for the reasons I have mentioned. Many of the wartime congregations would have benefited from the business the guards brought to the shops, cafés, restaurants and tradesmen.

What about those who didn't play a pivotal role in the murders and after the war remained silent? In his book "Justice Delayed," David Cesarani, writing about early 1950s, stated: *"A silence descended over the history of the genocidal campaign against the Jews of Europe."* This was a silence, not just by perpetrators, but across the political and Christian spectrums as a whole. There were very few books written about The Holocaust at that time. The Nuremburg Trials had failed to stir up the interest they should have done. They were described as boring by journalists covering the court hearings. Britain had issues to deal with in Palestine but was allowing thousands of displaced foreign police officers and soldiers into the UK. These men had served with the German military or police units but did not want to return to Ukraine, Lithuania, Poland and Latvia because the Soviet Union was governing those nations. Many of these men were war criminals. Many bore the SS tattoo under their arms. Between 1945 and 1950, 114,000 Poles and 91,000 European voluntary workers were allowed entry into Britain to work and seek British citizenship.

Many of these immigrants were clearly involved in killing of Jews in their home nations but British examination boards were lax in the investigations regarding their wartime activities. Doctors and medical staff had seen the SS tattoos on these men who were granted UK entry. Yet only 2,000 displaced Jews were allowed UK entry and that was by way of the Distressed Relatives Scheme.

Meanwhile, 9,000 Ukrainian soldiers/police of the 14th Waffen SS Galizien division were allowed into Britain and to apply for British citizenship. These SS men had been involved in the killing of Jews. Archbishop Ivan Bucko, a Vatican official, supported their applications to stay in the UK. In May 1947 the former SS division recruits arrived in the UK, many of whom settled permanently in the country. Before the British European Voluntary Workers Programme ended in 1949 more than 10,000 ex-SS soldiers were allowed into Britain.

The Church remained silent over this policy. There were representations against this programme by a few politicians but the majority turned a blind eye. The only voice which did not remain silent was that of The Simon Wiesenthal Centre, which as the years progressed provided the Home Office with details of war criminals residing in the UK. One war criminal, Kyrylo Zvarich, a Ukrainian police officer who had served with German Waffen SS units in Ukraine and who had entered the UK just after the war, was subject to Russian as well as Wiesenthal interest. Vic Satzewich's book "The Ukrainian Diaspora" details the attempts by Russia to extradite Zvarich after finding him guilty of murdering Jews in the Ukraine. Extradition was refused by the British Government and Zvarich died in Bolton UK in 1986. There are many other similar examples.

Silence was also partly due to the fact that there was little sympathy with Jews in Britain despite the evidence about their horrific persecution during the war. This lack of sympathy was in part due to the skirmishes between British soldiers and Jewish extremists in Israel prior to the 1948 restoration of Israel as a state. The disorder happening in the Holy Land resulted in anti-Jewish riots in various UK cities. In 1947 slaughter house workers in Birkenhead refused to deal with animals destined for kosher butchers. In Cheetham Hill, Manchester, a Jewish community area, rioters smashed shop windows belonging to Jewish businesses and tore down the canopy of a synagogue. At the end of the 1947 August Bank Holiday arsonists set fire to a wooden synagogue in West Derby, Liverpool. There were also other anti-Jewish riots in Merseyside, Manchester, Glasgow, Bristol, Hull, Warrington and London. These riots were described by the then Home Secretary, James Chuter Ede, as simply hooliganism.

Silence by the Church was also an obvious result of complicity. However, after the war other issues which would not want publicity were emerging. Not only did many European Christians not want the world to know they had profited from the clearance and murder of Jews, but their clergy didn't want it to be known that they had encouraged the Final Solution or did nothing to stop genocide. Pope Pius X11 is now known as the Silent Pope as a direct consequence of clear and irrefutable evidence that he knew of the murders but failed to respond in a way which would help his fellow man.

After the war difficulties arose between Christians and Jews over parental rights of the Jewish children who had been rescued and fostered. Many disputes led to court battles over custody and parental rights. Many Christians refused to give back Jewish children they had concealed during the war because they claimed they were now Christian and not Jewish. In his book "Churches and the Holocaust," Mordicai Paldiel describes what happened in Holland after the war. There were 3,481 Jewish children known to have been rescued, of whom 2,041 were orphans. These orphans were subject of attempts by surviving relatives to have them reintegrated into their birth families. The dominant Christian view in Holland was that Christianity had replaced Judaism and that the Church had become the chosen people of God. Calvinist Christian Gesina Van der Molen, who had rescued Jewish children, led the battle in refusing to release the children. The Jewish community set up an organisation called "To the Child's Aid" and fought hard to have the children released. After a long battle all but 360 children were returned to their Jewish families.

Silence should not have been an option after the realisation of the atrocities of The Holocaust, but as previously stated, silence and denial are elements in the final stage of genocide.

Chapter 14 ~ What Next?

Are we again in danger of fuelling the fire under the cauldron of hatred, thereby enabling those who have a political and racial agenda to attempt another genocide? I have referred to an Anglican clergyman who has a history of vilifying Israel, and the Director of 'Embrace Middle East' who tries to demonstrate that Israel's policies are a danger to the Christians in Egypt. His 'Palestinianisation' of Jesus is also another factor in turning Christians away from our Jewish roots. Christian organisations such as Sabeel, Kairos, Hope University, the Church in Wales, and 400 Independent Welsh Churches are attempting to delegitimise Israel. They claim Israel is an occupying force and ultimately a danger to peace in the Middle East. Is Christendom preparing another attempt to destroy the people of God? If we accept that Christendom fuelled The Holocaust we must examine the nature of anti-Zionism or anti-Israel teaching within the Church today and the effect this is having.

Since the creation of the Jewish state on the 15th May 1948, those who taught that Israel had been replaced by the Church had to face up to the fact that biblical prophecies concerning Israel were being fulfilled and that God had not finished with this ancient nation. For the first time in 2000 years Jews could live in their own land, elect their own government, and speak the language of the Bible. They could do business in their own currency, the shekel, the biblical currency. They could keep the Torah, the Saturday Sabbath, and the biblical feasts which are God's calendar of worship. Jews are now able to show that God has never forsaken them.

The teaching that God has finished with Israel is heresy but it continues aplenty. Despite the fulfilment of prophecies of Jews returning to the land God promised them, many say Israel does not have a right to exist as an independent state or defend itself as other nations do. Church leaders disregard the prophecies concerning the return of Jews to Israel and continue to ignore aspects of Judaism which God has never abrogated. One way for replacement theologians to discredit the Jews is to claim they are imposters. This is despite laws in some European nations banning such statements. Teaching that Israel is an occupying force is promulgated by large sections of Christendom. Some denominations call for boycotts, sanctions and divestment against Israel and rail against its policies.

The working paper by the European Union Agency for Fundamental Rights (June 2012) states: "The ongoing political conflict between Israel and Palestine has played an important role in the development and expression of anti-Semitism in the contemporary period, leading some to speak of a 'new anti-Semitism,' sometimes also referred to as 'anti-Zionism.' This form of anti-Semitism is expressed in a system of beliefs, convictions and political activities focused around the conflict in the Middle East. In this belief system, Israeli Jews are charged with the ultimate responsibility for the fate of the peace process, with the conflict presented as embodying the struggle between good and evil, with Israeli Jews allocated the latter role."

Christian anti-Zionism is the new Christian anti-Semitism in a different guise and encompasses the elements which the EFA identifies in its report. Instead of saying that Jews are a danger in society, which is what Christian leaders in Europe said prior to and during The Holocaust, it is said by many Christian leaders that Israel is a danger to peace in the Middle East. This is an absolute lie in the same way as the teaching prior to The Holocaust, that Jews were bent on taking over the world and responsible for the 1920s financial collapse in Germany. Views that Israel is an occupying, aggressive and oppressive regime undermining the rights of Palestinian Arabs has a means of demonising Jews. It is done under the guise of politics when it is really racial hatred. Christian leaders prior to and during The Holocaust created fear of Jews. Followers were told that that Jews were leading them into financial collapse in the interests of Bolshevism and world domination.

Jesus Christ is increasingly portrayed as a Palestinian and not the Jewish rabbi that He was. The "Palestinianisation" of Middle East Christianity is a common theme amongst anti-Semitic Church leaders.

Why does this teaching of hate and fear of Jews continue within Christendom? Why do Christians remain silent when Jews or Israel are unjustly vilified? Why do Church leaders promulgate lies and misinformation so as to raise the level of hatred of Jews and Israel in their congregations? The outworking of this hate dogma is seen in many forms. It is influential in today's rise of anti-Semitism in the same way as it was before the Second World War. The danger of denominational leaders' heretical teachings is that their views are taken on board by subordinate clergy, Christian organisations and rank-and-file church members.

The 2013 European Agency for Fundamental Rights survey, which involved eight EU member states, including the UK, described the personal experiences of 5,847 Jews. On page 49 of the report a UK Jew in his mid-fifties said: *"I once had anti-Semitic graffiti on my locker at work. It was nasty stuff put there by a born again Christian."* This Christian must have formed his hatred of Jews from somewhere.

During the Christmas period of 2013 Hope University in Liverpool, the only ecumenical Christian university in Europe, staged an exhibition which vilified Israel. The local Jewish community and many local Bible-believing Christians were exasperated by the lack of immediate response by the university to resolve the issue. When we began to openly challenge the university one Jewish lady from the city wrote to me saying: *"My concerns about Hope University go deeper and further than this display due to conversations I have had with students, and ex-students, who have all studied social work at Hope University. I cannot explain how scared I feel at times living as a Jew in Liverpool. I cannot allow myself to think about the information that is shared and messages (overt and covert) delivered daily about Jewish people and the state of Israel across this city and other cities in the UK and Europe or I am in danger of becoming paralysed with fear."*

At the same time St. James's Church in Piccadilly, London, built a huge wall replicating a security scene in Israel. The wall, eight metres tall and 30 metres long, cost £30,000. It was so big it blotted out the view of the church building. The wall, unveiled by the Rector, was used as a central attraction for the Christmas festival. The wall was used to vilify Israel who is simply defending her citizens by erecting checkpoints, security walls and fences to successfully thwart terrorism attacks. The festival referred to its Israeli replica structure as an apartheid and separation wall. Will this Rector, who is a regular presenter on BBC "Word for Today" programme be remembered for the loving way in which she speaks about most members of mankind or for the way in which she incited hatred of Israel?

Well-known personalities within Christendom vilify Israel at Christian summer camps and conferences throughout the world. The same Western Christian leaders who vilify Israel ignore the fact that its democratic government is the only one in the Middle East that allows religious freedom. Christianity there is growing. They say little or nothing about the persecution of Christians elsewhere in the region. The accusations that

Israel's policies are the cause of political instability in the region, and for the shrinking of Christian communities in the Gaza Strip and Bethlehem, are nonsensical. These slurs mirror the lies of Christian leaders in the 1930s when ordinary people believed their lies. This resulted in ordinary people becoming mass murderers.

A new wave of anti-Semitism is emerging from the Church in the United States. As the USA Mega Church movement takes hold the next generation of Christians are being influenced by anti-Semitic clergy. Teaching on social justice for Palestinians is the major sermon topic. Manipulation of the facts about Israel and the scriptures is common. The wrong emphasis includes the misuse of Micah 6: 8 which says: *"He has told you, O mortal, what is good; and what does the LORD require of you but to do justice, and to love kindness, and to walk humbly with your God."* Of course we should seek justice but what about justice for Israelis?

This verse is used as a tool to condemn Israel. The Jewish state is accused of abusing the human rights of Palestinian Arabs. Critics say that Israel's "blockade" of Arab areas is the same as apartheid was in South Africa. Israel, of course, is simply trying to defend her citizens. Israel's enemies want to deny her right to self-defence and tell lies about military actions that have to be taken.

I have been on the wrong end of rocket fire from the Gaza Strip and close to suicide bombings in Haifa and Jerusalem. I have seen the consequences of terrorism for Israel's long-suffering communities as a result of such attacks. Some Christian leaders don't regard these attacks as terrorism. That is as much a lie as European Christian leaders' misinformation in the Nazi era when they said Jews were a danger to the Church and society.

We are saddened to hear of Palestinian Arabs who suffer from loss of life and property resulting from war or violence. Their plight is however a result of the actions of their own leadership not Israel.

However, Christian organisations, such as Sabeel and Christ at the Checkpoint, cry foul when Israel's military defensive actions kill Gazan women and children deployed by Hamas terrorists as human shields.

Arab communities receive financial support from Christian organisations and individual believers throughout Europe. This is despite the European Union admitting that the Palestinian Authority lost or wasted 1.92 billion euros in aid between 2012 and 2014.

Palestinian Arabs had a far higher standard of living under Israeli governance than they did under Egyptian and Jordanian rule. Their standard of living fell dramatically when the Palestinian Authority took control of the West Bank (Judea, Samaria and the Gaza Strip). Things are even worse since Hamas took control of the Gaza Strip. Theft of financial and material aid, and the teaching of hatred in the Palestinian Arab media and educational system have led to an increase in violence. Yet much of Christendom calls for punitive action against Israel, not the Palestinian Authority or Hamas, for what is taking place.

With a senior and highly respected UK Jewish lady I visited an Anglican bishop to challenge him about a statement he made condemning Israel for the deaths of children in the 2014 Gaza War. He told us his information, which was the basis of his condemnation, came from BBC broadcasts. The fact that this prelate condemned a nation on unsubstantiated news reports is a confirmation that the lessons of the past have not been learned. For a bishop to ask his governing body to accept the lie that Israel intentionally kills Arab children highlights the age we live in. His response is no different to the actions of European Bishops during the Holocaust.

The prophet Joel gives a staggering warning about a future judgment of nations. We will find ourselves on the wrong side if many denominational leaders have their way.

Joel 3:2-3 quotes God saying: "I will gather all the nations and bring them down to the valley of Jehoshaphat, and I will enter into judgment with them there, on account of my people and my heritage Israel, because they have scattered them among the nations. They have divided my land, and cast lots for my people, and traded boys for prostitutes, and sold girls for wine, and drunk it down."

Jesus repeats details of this judgment in Matthew 25: 31-46: "When the Son of Man comes in his glory, and all the angels with him, then he will sit on the throne of his glory. All the nations will be gathered before him, and he will separate people one from another as a shepherd separates the sheep from the goats, and he will put the sheep at his right hand and the goats at the left. Then the king will say to those at his right hand, 'Come, you that are blessed by my Father, inherit the kingdom prepared for you from the foundation of the world; for I was hungry and you gave me food, I was thirsty and you gave me something to drink, I was a stranger and you welcomed me, I was naked and you gave me clothing, I was sick and you took care of me, I was in prison and you visited me.' Then the righteous will answer him, 'Lord, when was it that we saw you hungry and gave you food, or thirsty and gave you something to drink? And when was it that we saw you a stranger and welcomed you, or naked and gave you clothing? And when was it that we saw you sick or in prison and visited you?' And the king will answer them, 'Truly I tell you, just as you did it to one of the least of these who are members of my family, you did it to me.' Then he will say to those at his left hand, 'You that are accursed, depart from me into the eternal fire prepared for the devil and his angels; for I was hungry and you gave me no food, I was thirsty and you gave me nothing to drink, I was a stranger and you did not welcome me, naked and you did not give me clothing, sick and in prison and you did not visit me.' Then they also will answer, 'Lord, when was it that we saw you hungry or thirsty or a stranger or naked or sick or in prison, and did not take care of you?' Then he will answer them, 'Truly I tell you, just as you did not do it to one of the least of these, you did not do it to me.' And these will go away into eternal punishment, but the righteous into eternal life."

These verses are all about how and why we should support Israel and the Jewish people. Don't be fooled or deceived by many preachers today who say these verses are not about Israel. We have been open to deception in the past and we have read about the consequences.

OUR GENERATION, OUR TIME

So what can be done by our generation? We must firstly accept the truth that Christendom has throughout its history, and throughout The Holocaust, fuelled Hitler's own form of anti-Semitism resulting in genocide. Armed with that truth we can move towards resolving contemporary issues. We cannot, however, simply make statements about Israel and Jewish life and believe that all will be well. We have to be proactive and mirror the rescuers in The Holocaust, not to simply note who they were and what they achieved, but to repeat their actions.

Holocaust rescuers were ordinary people from a variety of backgrounds. There were rescuers even in the Nazi party. Not all reached their goal of saving Jews, but their attempts to do so deserve an accolade. In this category was Kurt Gerstein, an Institute of Hygiene member who joined the Nazi party to see if the rumours about the death camps were true. When Gerstein was able to prove mass killings were taking place he provided the evidence to the British and Swedish governments. When they refused to take notice he reported the facts to the Roman Catholic and Lutheran Church authorities. When these denominations refused to act a despairing Gerstein committed suicide.

Similarly, Hannah Senesh, a Hungarian Jew who in 1939 went to live in Israel (made aliyah). She joined the British army in 1943 and volunteered to be parachuted behind enemy lines. On 7th June 1944, at the height of the Holocaust deportations, she entered Hungary with the intention of informing Hungarian Jews of Nazi plans to deport them for the purpose of execution. She was quickly arrested by police and in the following November was executed by firing squad. Throughout her 23 years of life she wrote many poems, including the following.

"My God, My God, I pray that these things never end,

The sand and the sea,

The rustle of the waters,

Lightning of the Heavens,

The prayer of Man."

There were those like Polish sewer system worker and convicted thief Leopold Socha. He used his knowledge of the sewers to hide 20 Jews. He risked his life and the lives of his family in doing so. At the end of the war 10 of the hidden Jews survived.

What all Holocaust rescuers had in common was awareness. They were aware of the plight that their Jewish neighbours and family members were in. They were aware of the humanity issues involved and saw Jews as human beings just like themselves. They were resourceful, using whatever skills and material was at hand to help the beleaguered Jews. They made the best use of contacts to effect rescues. Sympathy for those they wanted to rescue was part of their make-up.

Hannah Senesh had empathy as she grew up in the Hungarian Jewish community. Leopold Socha and Kurt Gerstein had sympathy for the Jews and hated injustice with a passion. They were vigilant. They knew who were friends and who were foes, and they also knew the risks involved for their families and for those they called on to help. They were inventive, thinking through all aspects of their plans, using instinct and acquired knowledge to devise ways to achieve their goals. They had courage and compassion to such a degree that they were willing to lay down their lives for others. They also had persistence and commitment, so much so that they would not stop until they had done all they could.

Today there are rescuers in Israel, men and women who give their lives to save others. Israel has world-class medical expertise which is not only used to save the lives of Jews and Arabs living in the Holy Land but Palestinians Arabs living in Gaza and Palestinian Authority controlled areas. There are two Arab teenagers from Gaza who receive life-saving dialysis 12 hours a day in Rambam Hospital, Haifa. Ahmed Hamdan and his sister Hadeel have been receiving free medical support since 2012.

In 2015, the Israeli defence unit responsible for Palestinian civilian affairs, Cogat, said that well before the yearend it had granted about 27,000 medical permits for Gazans to travel for care in Israel, Judea and Samaria (West Bank), and neighbouring Jordan. That number includes patients and relatives accompanying patients.

A different type of rescue is also taking place in Israel, and that is by individuals protecting their families and neighbours from the many thousands of rockets which have been fired at them since 2000. An example of love and care to all of us is Ella Abukasis, a 17-year-old Jewish girl from Sderot. This town close to the Gaza Strip has been the frequent target of rockets fired by militants across the border since the Intifada (uprising) of 2000.

On the afternoon of 15th January 2005 Ella was walking home from a family birthday celebration with her 11-year-old brother Tamir when a rocket from Gaza was fired. An alarm was sounded giving a 20-second warning to take cover. There was no shelter nearby so brave Ella used her body to shield her brother. As they lay on the ground the rocket exploded nearby. Shrapnel penetrated Ella's head and also left her brother slightly injured. Ella died in hospital on 21st January having given her life to save her brother. This was the sacrifice of one who loved so deeply that she sacrificed her life to save the younger brother in her care.

Our generation must similarly show love and care by countering the rising incitement to hate Israel in and outside the Church. We must reflect on the past and learn the lesson that being a bystander is not an option. European churches in a multiplicity of denominations incited hatred towards the Jews even before Hitler achieved power in Germany. They taught that

Jews were a danger to society. This was clearly a lie but those sitting in the pews were bamboozled into believing the message.

Many Christians have little or no idea about the plethora of Scriptural prophecies regarding the Promised Land of Israel and God's future plans for the Jewish people. My experience of teaching about fulfilled and future biblical prophecies and giving an analysis of history has shown that mind-sets of those totally opposed to Israel can be changed. Even British National Party supporters have moved from hating of Jews to supporting them. While Palestinian Arabs have rights, it must be emphasised that Israel has a right to exist and live in peace within secure borders. Israel has many roles to fulfil in the modern world including a spiritual one. There is a great need for those who support Israel to plough more resources into educating people about this remarkable young nation that has already become a world leader in several scientific fields.

Prior to and during the Holocaust, Christian leaders preached messages of hate. We must vehemently oppose those who do so today. Being outspoken can be a difficult thing to do but my experience, and those of others, shows that it will have a positive impact. We must remember that silence is not an option, for it may be understood as an indication of support for those who are inciting hatred.

The written word is important. Writing letters and supporting pro-Israel organisations is a given. Writing comments on web sites is an important job to educate those seeking a greater knowledge of Holy Land facts. I've found that writing letters to MPs and MEPs is effective.

The book of Lamentations has strong messages for today. The word lamentations means "how" or "alas!" We have seen how The Holocaust developed, and if all we can say is "alas!" when Israel is vilified that is not good enough for God. "Alas!" is for bystanders not rescuers.

Lamentations 1:2 states: "She weeps bitterly in the night, with tears on her cheeks; among all her lovers she has no one to comfort her; all her friends have dealt treacherously with her, they have become her enemies."

Many in Christendom are living with what appears to be an idyllic memory of our role in Holocaust. However it is not at all ideal and in reality it is a dangerous memory as if we won't learn from our horrific past we will repeat it. We must not leave it any longer to let our generation and particularly the younger generation know the truth about the past and remove this Idyllic amnesia which will, if we allow it, repeat past evils. Let us in Christendom, who are truly Israel's friends, never again deal treacherously with her or be silent. Let us oppose incitement to hate God's chosen people with all that we have. Incitement which leads to hatred leads to violence and ultimately Genocide.

As informative as this book is it is as much of a warning that we have to tell the truth about what we did in Christendom to fuel and enable the Holocaust. We have without doubt the blood of millions of Jews on our hands.

Today we have a choice. The prophet Ezekiel was told to give a message to Israel. If he failed to give the warning he would suffer. If he gave the warning and the people ignored it they would suffer. "Mortal, I have made you a sentinel for the house of Israel; whenever you hear a word from my mouth, you shall give them warning from me. If I say to the wicked, "You shall surely die," and you give them no warning, or speak to warn the wicked from their wicked way, in order to save their life, those wicked persons shall die for their iniquity; but their blood I will require at your hand. But if you warn the wicked, and they do not turn from their wickedness, or from their wicked way, they shall die for their iniquity; but you will have saved your life". **Ezekiel 3:17-19 (NRSV)**

I pray that we will all be sentinels for the house of Israel and for the Jewish communities who live amongst us and enrich our lives.

Your Next Step

How can YOU get involved to prevent the hatred spreading?

Father's House Sabbath Congregation is a Christian congregation committed to support Jews in the UK and in Israel. The proceeds from this publication goes to the congregation to help them reach these goals.

The congregation has a programme of educating Christians and the Secular about the biblical mandate for the Jewish people, their history and their future inheritance. This programme takes the form of a seven-module course which has been taught throughout the UK, Eire, Holland, Germany and Lithuania and Belarus.

We are able to train those who would like to become teachers of this programme in their own area. The course has been translated into Dutch and Belarussian. The course has seen some who had antisemitic views such as some members of the British National Party change their opinions entirely. There is clear evidence that education can help prevent hate.

Father's House is very active in its support of Jewish events and advocates for Israel in a number of forums including street advocacy. The Congregation holds Holocaust Exhibitions and helps others to do the same.

If you would like me to come to your area and speak please contact me at Father's House.

If you would like to join us in these and other activities, which are all aimed at reducing hatred in our nation, then please CONTACT US using the details below:

www.FathersHouse.wales

www.facebook.com/fathershousesc

fathershousecongregation@gmail.com

Phone (UK): 01244 823 378   (Int'l): +44-1244 823 378

About the Author

Pastor Michael Fryer

Mike Fryer is a retired National Crime Squad Detective and is now a pastor of Father's House Sabbath Congregation in North Wales and founder of Christian for Zion UK.

Father's House is a congregation which follows The Lords Festivals including Sabbath with passionate Worship and a strong emphasis on the word. Father's House also works alongside the Jewish Community in Israel and the UK to build strong relationships.

Mike graduated in Holocaust Studies in 2009, having studied over a period of 4 years at Yad Vashem. He is a regular visitor to Israel, particularly to the Southern towns, who are regularly bombarded with rockets from Gaza. Mike teaches on the Sabbath, The Lords Feasts, the period of the False Messiah and Christian anti-Semitism including Paganism in the Church.

Mike has written a number of booklets to help us understand the Feasts, Sabbath and some of the issues surrounding our Christian practice. He also wrote a small book on dealing with the occult and Wiccan practice in Wales. In 2000 Mike wrote the Hidden Treasure Course, a seven session course about Israel which he, along with a team of teachers, teach throughout the UK, Ireland, Europe and Russia. The course is repeated regularly on Revelation TV.

Mike's heart is to help the church find its Jewish identity through education and encouragement and to help all in Christendom, understand our past with the aim of preventing the return of the antisemitism/antizionism of old which resulted in the Holocaust amongst other atrocities.

About the Publisher

WRITE your book.
BUILD your brand.
CREATE your platform.
BROADCAST your message.
EXPAND your reach and income...

Perissos Media helps business owners, speakers, consultants, professionals, sales teams, ministry leaders and inspired individuals to PUBLISH books, audio and video training products and other marketing materials.

Our goal is to BUILD your platform and ELEVATE you to "expert status" in your field—with all the financial and lifestyle benefits that come with it.

Personally, I have had the great pleasure and honor of working with a number of talented business owners, public speakers and ministers on a variety of projects from start to finish. We start with dialogue and planning, and then we organize recorded interviews, transcription, editing, formatting, cover design, branding and numerous marketing strategies.

What we produce is a PLATFORM for influential people to expand their reach thorough books and workbooks, audio and video training packages, speaking engagements and a global PRESENCE on Amazon, Google, social media and beyond.

For a **FREE copy of one of our Amazon books** to help you to publish your message to a greater audience, please visit:

www.IWantToPublish.com

We look forward to serving you,

Jerry Kuzma

Director, PerissosGroup.com

Bibliography

"A Convenient Hatred" *Phyllis Goldstein*. Published by Facing History and ourselves National Foundation USA 2012.
ISBN 978-09819543-8-7

"A Guest at the Shooters Banquet" *Rita Cabis*. Published by Bloomsbury books 2015.
ISBN 987-1-63286-261-7

"A History of the Jewish People" edited by *H.H.Ben-Sasson* Published by Dvir Publishing House , Tel Aviv 1969.
ISBN 0-674-39731-2

"A Moral Reckoning" by *Daniel Jonah Goldhagen*. Published by Alfred A Knopf 2002.
ISBN 0-349-11693-8

"ANTI-SEMITISM- The Longest Hatred" by *Robert S. Wistrich*. Published by Methuen of London 1991.
ISBN 0-413-65320-X

"Atlas of the Holocaust" *Martin Gilbert*. Published by Michael Joseph Ltd. 1982.
ISBN 0-7181-2160-0

"Churches and the Holocaust" *Mordecai Paldiel*. Published by KTAV publishing House,Inc.2006.
ISBN 0-88125-908-X

"Days of Ruin" *Raz Segal*. Published by Yad Vashem 2013.
ISBN 978-965-308-428-5

"Documents on the Holocaust" edited by *Yitzhak Arad, Israel Gutman and Abraham Margaliot.* Published by University of Nebraska Press 1999.
ISBN 965-308-078-4

"Gleams of Memory" by **Michael Treister**. Published by The Minsk Historical Workshop 2011.
No ISBN

"From Ambivalence to Betrayal" by **Robert S. Wistrich**. Published by University of Nebraska Press 2012.
ISBN 978-0-8032-4076--6
"History of the Holocaust" by **Yehuda Bauer**. Published by Franklyn Watts a division of Grolier Publishing 1982.
ISBN 0-531-05641-4

"Hitler and the Holocaust" **Robert Wistrich**. Published by Phoenix Paperback 2001.
ISBN 1-84212-486-2

"Hitler's Wiling Executioners" **Daniel Jonah Goldhagen**. Published ABACUS 1996.
ISBN 978-0-349-10786-8

"Hunt for the Jews" by **Jan Grabowski**. Published by Indiana University Press 2013.
ISBN 978-0-253-01074-2

"IBM and the Holocaust" by **Edwin Black**. Published by Time Warner Paperback 2002.
ISBN 0-7515-3199-5

"In the Shadow of Death" by **Joseph Foxman**. Published by United States Holocaust Museum 2011.
ISBN 978-0-9814686-5-5

"Justice Delayed" by **David Cesarani**. Published by Pheonix Press
ISBN 1 84212 126 X

"Occupation Nazi Hunter" **Efraim Zuroff**. Published by Ashford Press Publishing 1988.
ISBN 1-85253-108-8

"Ordinary Men" **Christopher R. Browning**. Published by Penguin books 2001.
ISBN 13; 978-0-14-100042-8

"Poland's Holocaust" by **Tadeusz Piotrowski**. Published by McFarland & Company, Inc., Publishers 1998.
ISBN 0-7864-0371-3

"Ponary Diary" Edited by **Yitzhak Arad**. Published by Towarzystwo Milosnikow, Wilna Ziemi Wilnskiej and Rachel Margolis 1999.
ISBN 978-0-300-10853-8

"Surviving the Holocaust" by **Avraham Tory**. Published by Harvard University Press 1990.
ISBN 0-7126-5033-4

"The Holocaust and the Christian World" by **Carol Rittner, Stephen D Smith and Irena Steinfeldt**. Published by Kuperard of Bravo Ltd. 2000.
ISBN 1-85733277-6

"The Italians and the Holocaust" **Susan Zuccotti.** Published by Peter Halban Publishers Ltd. 1987.
ISBN 1-870015-03-7

"The Jews in Poland" Edited by **Chimen Abramsky,Maciej Jachimczyk and Anthony Polonsky**. Published by Basil Blackwell Ltd.1986.
ISBN 0-631-16582-7

"The Popes against the Jews" **David Kertzer**. Published by Vintage books 2001.
ISBN 0-375-40623-9

"The Secret Wars against the Jews" by **John Loftus and Mark Aarons**. Published by St. Martin's Press 1994.
ISBN 0-312-11057-X

"The Terrible Secret" *Walter Laqueur*, Published by Penguin books 1980.
ISBN 0-1400-6136-3

"The Twisted Cross" *Doris L Bergen*. Published by University of North Carolina Press1996.
ISBN 978-0-8078-2253-1

"Trials of the Diaspora by *Anthony Julius*". Published by Oxford University Press 2010
ISBN 978-0-19-929705-4

 "The Holocaust in the Soviet Union" by *Yitzak Arad*. Published by the University of Nebraska Press 2009.
ISBN 978-0-8032-2059-1

"Unholy Trinity" by *Mark Aarons and John Loftus*. Published by St. Martin's Press 1991.
ISBN 0-312-07111-6

END NOTES

[i] Alexander Charles Carlile, Lord Carlile of Berriew CBE QC FRSA, Hansard Debate, House of Commons, 19th Nov 1990.

[ii] Kazimierz Sakowicz, Yitzhak Arad, Ed., *Blurb of Ponary Diary, 1941-1943, A Bystander's Account of a Mass Murder*, (Yale University Press: 2005).

[iii] Mordecai Paldiel, Churches and the Holocaust: Unholy Teaching, Good Samaritans, and Reconciliation, (New Jersey: KTAV Publishing House Inc., 2006) p.179

[iv] Randolph M Braham, *The Christian Churches of Hungary and the Holocaust*, Yad Vashem Studies, Vol. 29, Jerusalem (2001), p. 4. http://www1.yadvashem.org/odot_pdf/Microsoft%20Word%20-%202278.pdf Accessed 27 January 2016.

[v] Braham, The Christian Churches of Hungary and the Holocaust, p. 14. http://www1.yadvashem.org/odot_pdf/Microsoft%20Word%20-%202278.pdf Accessed 7 February 2016.

[vi] Branham, The Christian Churches of Hungary and the Holocaust, pp. 32-33.
Accessed 27 January 2016.

[vii] Yitzhak Arad, *The Christian Churches and the Persecution of Jews in the Occupied Territories of the U.S.S.R.*, p.4. http://www.yadvashem.org/odot_pdf/Microsoft%20Word%20-%203235.pdf Accessed 7 February 2016
from C Rittner, S C Smith, & I Steinfeldt, eds, *The Holocaust and the Christian World – Reflections on the past, Challenges for the Future*, (London: Kuperard Publication, 2000), pp. 108-111.

[viii] Arad, The Christian Churches and the Persecution of Jews in the Occupied Territories of the U.S.S.R., p.4.
Accessed 7 February 2016
from The Holocaust and the Christian World – Reflections on the past, Challenges for the Future, (London: Kuperard Publication, 2000), pp. 108-111.

[ix] *Croatia 2012 International Religious Freedom Report*, International Religious Freedom Report for 2012 United States Department of State • Bureau of Democracy, Human Rights and Labor, p.5.
http://www.state.gov/documents/organization/208512.pdf Accessed 7 February 2016

[x] War Crimes Bill, (Hansard, 19 March, 1990), *Vol 169, cc889-977.*
http://hansard.millbanksystems.com/commons/1990/mar/19/war-crimes-bill   Accessed 7 February 2016

[xi] Eva Fogelman, *Conscience and Courage,* (Knopf Doubleday Publishing Group, 17 Aug 2011) np.

[xii] Kenneth Stow, *Popes, Church, and Jews in the Middle Ages: Confrontation and Response. (*Ashgate Press, 2007), pp. 57–58.
ISBN 0-7546-5915-1.

[xiii] Anthony J Scolio, The Holocaust, the Church, and the Law of Unintended Consequences: How Christian Anti-Judaism Spawned Nazi Anti-Semitism, A Judge's Verdict, (iUniverse, 7 April 2014), p. 65.

[xiv] Scolio, The Holocaust, the Church, and the Law of Unintended Consequences, p. 66.
[xv] Wills Garry, *Structures of Deceit: Papal Sin.* (London: Darton, Longman & Todd, 2000), p.37

[xvi] David I Kertzer, Unholy War: The Vatican's Role in the Rise of Modern Anti-semitism, (Pan Macmillan, 2003), p. 138.

[xvii] Victor Marsden, Translation from Russian, *The Protocols of the Learned Elders of Zion*, (Book Tree, 1999) np.

[xviii] Robert Michael, A History of Catholic Antisemitism: The Dark Side of the Church, (Palgrave MacMillan, 2008), p .201.

[xix] Susan Zuccotti, The Italians and the Holocaust: Persecution , Rescue and Survival, (Univ. of Nebraska Press, 1987), p. 31.

[xx] David I Kertzer, The Pope and Mussolini: The Secret History of Pius XI and the Rise of Facism in Europe, (OUP Oxford, 2014), p. 196.

[xxi] Kertzer, *Unholy War,* p. 273.

[xxii] Kertzer, *Unholy War,* p. 147.

[xxiii] Kertzer, *Unholy War,* p. 7.

[xxiv] Susan Zuccotti, Under His Very Windows: The Vatican and the Holocaust in Italy, (Yale University Press, 2002), p. 12.

[xxv] Kertzer, Unholy War, p. 278. citing Mario Barbera "Intorno alla questione del sionismo", Civilta Cattolica, 1938, II, pp. 76-82

[xxvi] John Henry Newman, *Essay on the Development of Christian Doctrine,* a Cardinal by Pope Leo III in 1879, 1878, p351-353. http://www.bible.ca/trinity/trinity-Newman.htm Accessed 29/4/16

[xxvii] Robert Michael, Luther, Luther Scholars and the Jews: Encounter 46:4 (Autumn 1985), p. 342.

[xxviii] United States Holocaust Memorial Museum. "Introduction to the Holocaust." Holocaust Encyclopedia. *Adolph Hitler the Early Years 1889-1913.* www.ushmm.org/wlc/en/article.php?ModuleId=10005143 Accessed on 29/2/16

[xxix] Mark Aarons and John Loftus. *Unholy Trinity: The Vatican, The Nazis, and the Swiss Bankers.* (New York: St. Martin's Press, 1991; revised, 1998)/ Chapter 2, np.

[xxx] Zuccotti, Under His Very Windows, p. 1.

[xxxi] Robert Wistrich, *Hitler and the Holocaust,* (Hachette UK: 2013), np.

[xxxii] Phyllis Goldstein, Harold Evans, *A Convenient Hatred: The History of Anti-Semitism,* (Facing History and Ourselves: 2012), np.

[xxxiii] Susan Zuccotti, The Italians and the Holocaust: Persecution ,Rescue and Survival, (University of Nebraska Press: 1987) p. 129.

[xxxiv] Daniel Weis, *Everlasting Wisdom,* (Paragon Publishing: 2010), p. 81.

[xxxv] Jan Grabowski, Hunt for the Jews: Betrayal and Murder in German Occupied Poland, (Indianan University Press: 2013), p. 20.

[xxxvi] Grabowski, *Hunt for the Jews,* p. 84.

[xxxvii] Grabowski, *Hunt for the Jews,* p. 83.

[xxxviii] Grabowski, *Hunt for the Jews,* p. 20.

[xxxix]Report by Waffen SS on Killing of Jews in the Pripet Marshes, from 27th July to 11th August 1941, (Shoah Resource Centre). http://www.yadvashem.org/odot_pdf/Microsoft%20Word%20-%205318.pdf Accessed 2 March 2016.

[xl] Walter Laqueur, The Terrible Secret: Suppression of the Truth about Hitler's Final Solution, (Transaction Publishers: 2012), p. 176.

[xli] Victoria J Barnett, *The Role of the Churches: Compliance and Confrontation,* Dimensions, Vol 12, No. 2, 1998 (ADL Braun Holocaust Institute: 1998)

archive.adl.org/braun/dim_14_1_role_church.html. Accessed 2 March 2016.

[xlii] Winston Churchill, uncovered in 2007 by Cambridge University Historian, Dr Richard Toyne,
How the Jews Can Combat Persecution. 1937.
www.cam.ac.uk/...uncovered-the-"lost"-paper-churchill=kept-from-publication Accessed 2 March 2016.

Lightning Source UK Ltd.
Milton Keynes UK
UKOW05f2314271016
286353UK00003B/192/P